VOICES OF Impact

EMPOWERING STORIES FROM FEMALE VISIONARIES AND ENTREPRENEURS

Voices of Impact Publishing

Copyright © 2022 Voices Of Impact Publishing

Foreword by Melanie Wood

All rights reserved. No part of this publication may be reproduced, stored in a retrieval system, or transmitted in any form or by any means, electronic, mechanical, photocopying, recording or otherwise, without the prior written permission from both the copyright owner and publisher.

Disclaimer

All the information, techniques, skills, and concepts contained within this publication are of the nature of general comment only and are not in any way recommended as individual advice. The intent is to offer a variety of information to provide a wider range of choices now and in the future, recognising that we all have widely diverse circumstances and viewpoints. Should any reader choose to make use of the information contained herein, this is their decision and the author and publishers do not assume any responsibilities whatsoever under any condition or circumstances.

Foreword by Melanie Wood

Stories are the most powerful way to have an impact and create a ripple effect in this world.

I have worked with hundreds of women to gain Clarity and Confidence in sharing their stories on stage, on podcasts, at summits and more.

An opportunity came to me early in 2022 to create this book series to share transformational stories of women making an impact. Sharing my own story in 2020 in a book series and becoming a best-selling author was a game changer. It was time to give this opportunity to other women to make an impact.

It began as something I'd never set out to do; I wasn't born a speaker, a leader or a business owner. Throughout my life, public speaking was never on my horizon. I would avoid it throughout school and my career for almost thirty years – and I did well to avoid it at all costs!

Not setting out to do what I do today came from one of my biggest challenges back in my late teens and early 20s. I was in an abusive marriage where I lost my confidence, voice, certainty, my way in life, and who I was as a woman to the point that I didn't want to be here.

Then one day, a person came along and gave me hope. She reached out to me on a day I couldn't hide anymore what I was going through, and she asked if I was okay, and for once, I said, "No." I knew I had to be ok with using my voice and what would happen next. Her "Impact" on my life is why I'm here today and why I'm so passionate about sharing stories.

As she shared her own story, it gave me hope and the support I needed to leave that marriage. After meeting her and the years that followed, I knew that I was here for more to help other women overcome challenges and find their voice, confidence, and certainty around who they are.

Life changed for me one day 9yrs ago; an opportunity to come to Australia for a year, and something within told me it was time for my adventure to begin, which was what I had been waiting for. Before leaving, I was given the book "The Secret" by Rhonda Byrne. Which changed the way I viewed the world at that moment.

Arriving in Australia, I was ready! Ready to take action! Even though I was scared of being in a new country, I built my new life to stay permanently in Australia. I wanted to help women like you (that amazing lady reading this book!) have a voice, confidence and clarity. To be able to use your authenticity to create and build a skill set for you and your business and your life or represent your organisation through storytelling, public speaking and communication.

I started my business, Speaking Styles, five years ago and have worked with hundreds of women to help them have a voice in this world to share their story, their message, and their value. To be heard and understood in this world and create a ripple effect, as I believe that stories are how we save lives, make a change, heal ourselves, and help heal other people—giving them hope and permission to do the same.

Building my business for the past 5yrs and working with women is because I knew how to use speaking to create an impact and attract clients. Out of my past experience, I understand what it's like to be in my client's shoes to have empathy and authenticity to work and guide them through sharing their stories.

Doing this work didn't come without its challenges; over 2 years ago, I was 3 days out from living in my car when the big C hit; 6 months before that, I was in debt and struggling to have enough money for rent and food.

I knew these challenges and feelings were part of who I was becoming and where I would be of service in this world—being heartfelt and authentic in everything I do. I didn't get here on my own; yes, I've done the work of the people who have worked with me and guided me over the past 5yrs, and without them, this wouldn't be possible.

I know in my heart that sharing stories is how we create change and save the lives of others, heal ourselves and rise all of us as a collective. By sharing your story, by communicating your message, by communicating your fantastic work, experience, and expertise, no matter what field you are in. Just like the 25 women in this book are sharing.

At the beginning of the year, I had this burning desire to create a new opportunity for women to share their transformational stories and IMPACT the world on a larger scale and reach more people. Then one day, only a few months ago, that opportunity came knocking, and Voices of Impact was born, and that desire came to light.

In the past 3 months, 25 women said yes to being published authors, and it has been an absolute pleasure to publish incredible women's transformational stories.

In Volume 1 of Voices of Impact, you will read 25 Visionary Women from around the world sharing TRANSFORMATIONAL stories, creating change and a ripple effect in this WORLD. Change is within each of us, waiting to be heard and understood.

Ladies, it's your time to step up, step out and lead the change! The world needs to hear your story!

IMPACT starts with you. Are you with me?

Melanie Wood
Founder, Speaker, Author, Publisher
Voices of Impact Publishing

***

Would you love to have your voice heard to share your story?

Reach out x

melanie@speakingstyles.com.au

Contents

Colleen Dwyer 1

Jaime Lee Foord 15

Dr Dee Hacking 25

Chrissy Harris 39

Donna Kirkland 53

Faye Lawrence 65

Christine Lennon 79

Karen Macvicar 91

Cattalia Lee Montgomery 103

Jodi Porteous 117

Dori Stewart 129

Sharon L Bech 141

Katie Chapman 153

Dr Carolyn Daniels 165

Najma Khan 179

Natalie Lewis 193

Alissa Meechan 207

Kären Moroney 219

Susie Moore 233

Lorrayne Robbinz 247

Dr Libby Roesner 259

Vicki Tate 273

Danni Vee 287

Camilla Ward 299

Rhonda Whiteley 313

Colleen Dwyer

"Do you have any employees?" the message read.

After commenting on one of her social media posts, I was chatting with a woman who had reached out and asked if I could give her any advice. She had started up her own cleaning business and needed help navigating the murky waters of employing others: Superannuation, Workcover, wages etc.

"I have about a dozen employees who are cleaners plus three admin staff – two are part-time, and I've recently hired a full-time manager. The business started out with only me nearly ten years ago.' I typed my answer quickly into my phone and hit send. "That's brilliant – what an achievement", she replied.

I smiled as I considered the words on the screen. I'd had so many challenges along the way, and I guess it was an achievement to be proud of. I couldn't help but wonder, "how did I get here?"

Before I go on with this short history, let me make a general observation – the test of first-rate intelligence is the ability to hold two opposed ideas in the mind at the same time, and still retain the ability to function.

> One should, for example, be able to see that things are hopeless and yet be determined to make them otherwise.
>
> ~ F. Scott Fitzgerald, The Crack-Up

Born in Sydney, New South Wales, I was the youngest daughter of Margaret Helen Bishop. Margaret had survived significant physical, mental and sexual abuse in government institutions as a child and the trauma that she suffered eventually manifested itself into a lifetime of addiction, crime and recovery. I have never been told who my biological father is, but modern DNA testing unveiled some of the mystery, revealing I had inherited significant Scottish, Irish, English and surprisingly Middle Eastern ethnicities. My, how the plot thickened and the void inside of me felt somewhat smaller when I could trace back my ancestry with that information.

With my birth mother fighting her own demons, I would eventually be adopted by Kathie, her younger sister, who married her childhood sweetheart, Allan. They had one son together and officially adopted my older sister and I in 1981, raising us all as one big happy family.

Dad was in the army, and we were a typical military family in 1980s Australia. My parents were strict, but fun and I have wonderful memories from when our family was together. My childhood at the time felt extraordinarily unremarkable, except for the fact we moved a lot. I attended seven different schools across three states. Always being the new kid, I felt like an alien everywhere I went; however, I always excelled at school, enjoying writing and poetry and I had a career in architecture planned out from an early age, so I studied graphic design throughout high school. I was obsessed with home design and would happily sit for hours designing my latest vision or mentally renovating most homes I walked into. As much as I disliked changing schools, I loved travelling to new places and moving into different houses.

My plan to study architecture at university in Brisbane unravelled one fateful morning in my senior high school year after an argument with my mother. I was sixteen and six months exactly and was excited to get my Learners Permit that day but was upset to learn she wouldn't be taking me to my test. Belligerently, I refused to get out of bed or go to school, embarrassed by the fact I wouldn't be getting my licence that day as I had said I would. When my exasperated mother challenged me to "get up and go to school or get a job", I did exactly that. My impulsive teenage brain "ruined everything", and six months before I should have been graduating, I was a high school dropout looking for a job. My poor mum once confessed she felt bad about it for years. Having teenagers myself now, I could completely understand how difficult it was for her and never held it against her.

My first job was serving Devonshire teas and flipping burgers to tourists in a small café near home. I was not a fan of the burger business and soon took an opportunity to work 20km away. It was around then that my parents' marriage of seventeen years ended, and subsequently, my Mum moved out, leaving just my dad, my brother and I behind. Without a driver's licence or a car and with no public transport available, I was unable to get myself to work. I found myself, at the tender age of seventeen, packing everything I owned into a small trailer and leaving home, bound for the bright lights and sandy beaches of Queensland's Gold Coast. Welcome to adulthood, Colleen.

Despite the fact that I owned very few material possessions, I was quite partial to this living out of the home business and quickly became accustomed to living independently. It never ceased to amaze me how easily I could make friends as an adult. As the new kid at school, I had always felt shy and awkward.

I wanted things to happen for me, but with no plan or guidance, I was relying heavily on the direction of the tide and the force of the wind to get me wherever I was going. Ambitious by design, I enrolled in short courses at TAFE and had a fascinating variety of occupations throughout my late teens and twenties. I was always employed full-time in an office with a second job on weekends in pubs and nightclubs, doing promotions, giving away prizes or working behind the bar. There was always an abundance of opportunities, and I was always optimistic. These jobs were my education, and the tuition I was receiving was invaluable.

When I was 27, with a string of failed relationships and a significant heartbreak behind me, I decided it was time to "get my shit together", so I enrolled in college to study for a Diploma in Software Development. At the time, I was typing radiology reports during the week and working at the local RSL club on weekends. In my spare time, I liked to water ski and wakeboard, so when the opportunity presented itself, it was natural for me to put my hand up to be the secretary and treasurer of our Water Ski Club as well. And boy, did I love to party!

Enter Life Changing Moment. I'm pregnant. Fuck.

We'd only been seeing each other for a few months when I knocked on the door of my boyfriend's unit to deliver the news. I wanted to talk about options. While I didn't not want to have kids, they certainly weren't on my agenda at that time.

I'd had a termination when I was 18 and after an abnormal pap-smear had been treated for CIN 1 and endometriosis in my early twenties, so after a considerable amount of reflection and contemplation, we decided this might be my only chance to have a baby (spoiler alert: it wasn't) and decided to keep it. Fast forward nine months, it's 2004, I'm engaged, and my beautiful daughter enters the world, making me a Mum for the first time.

By the end of the year, we were married, and I was back at work typing radiology reports. It soon became apparent I couldn't juggle working, studying and having a baby without suffering from terrible guilt if I was giving attention to one and not the other, so I made the decision to keep my job, ditch the studies and focus on being a mum.

In 2006, we welcomed our second baby into the world – a beautiful little boy. We also started a side hustle creating and editing real estate videos. We had researched and purchased everything we would need to start making money – the video camera, accessories and software. I was now juggling part-time work, a baby, a toddler and our own business. Maybe it just fizzled, or maybe it was the lack of passion (and experience!), but the video editing business never took off. It had sparked something in me, though, and I enrolled into a twelve-month TAFE course to study Multimedia, specifically web and graphic design and video editing.

While I was studying, I discovered I was pregnant again. I was excited to take my children along to my 12-week scan to surprise them with pictures of the baby. I worked at the practice I was having my scan at, so I knew exactly what I was looking at when my baby wasn't moving. I asked the sonographer what was wrong, even though I knew the answer. I had suffered a miscarriage. Speechless, he left the room, taking my kids from the room to the solace of my workmates as my heart broke, somebody came in to console me, but I don't remember who. I was devastated.

I returned to my studies, and after I completed my course started a web design business. At this time, my husband took an opportunity for an entry-level mining job in Parkes in New South Wales, about 1000km away. I stayed at home juggling the children, work and my web design side hustle. After only a couple of months, the GFC hit, and he was made redundant. I stopped creating websites and tried to focus once more on just being a mother with a normal job while my husband once again looked for work.

Financially we would always just get by, living from week to week. We had the obligatory car loan, credit cards and interest-free loans with no savings. We would talk about buying a home all the time, but we didn't know how to save and would argue over money constantly, mostly over what I was spending.

Despite my best efforts not to be, I fell pregnant once again, and my husband found employment in the mines. I was left at home once more, this time with three kids, welcoming our baby girl into the world just a few months after he started flying in and out to work. On maternity leave, I started typing radiology reports from home, and I also started playing around with informational websites based on the concept of Google ad words – attracting visitors based on keywords purely for the sake of generating income from ad clicks.

Eventually, we made the decision to move to Central Queensland, and I resigned from my position in radiology after 12 years of service, never returning from maternity leave.

Moving from the Gold Coast to the Central Queensland Coast in 2011 was a culture shock, to say the least. Even though I had agreed to it, I was fast becoming resentful that we had moved, leaving my dearest friends and their families behind.

Still looking for something else where he could work for himself, my husband heard about a franchise opportunity cleaning air conditioners and after researching this business concept, we decided we could start something similar ourselves.

We decided on the name Clean and Cleaner, and I went to work building a website, designed the business cards and started advertising. I loved a challenge.

I enjoyed developing and marketing the business, and soon the phone began to ring. But only once or twice was it for an air conditioner clean. The rest of the time, the enquiries came from people asking about house cleaning, which I turned down with a friendly apology. It didn't occur to me to say yes. Until one day, something changed.

A woman had called desperately seeking help to clean her home. After empathising with her predicament, I turned her down politely and ended the call. I don't know what made me change my mind that day, but I called her back to offer my help. I had always kept a very clean house and was a little obsessed with cleaning products, so I packed the essentials into the back of the car and voila! All of a sudden, I was a house cleaner. Didn't see that coming. And I loved it. I loved everything about it.

The birth of Clean and Cleaner coincided with the end of my marriage, and by 2014 I was a single parent and sole trader, facing challenges many single parents around the world face while also growing a small business. I was running the business alone, so it was the logical choice for me to hold onto it during our divorce, as it was my only source of income.

Struggling financially as a single parent, I had no choice but to succeed. I threw myself into the promotion of Clean and Cleaner, and if anyone asked me how my "little business" was going, I would wax lyrical about the highs and lows of small business before realising they were just being polite. I had always been independent, and I was unapologetically passionate about promoting my business.

> ❝
> The best way to find yourself is to lose yourself in the service of others.
> ~ Mahatma Gandhi

As I struggled to meet demand, I started hiring employees and immediately began noticing a worrying trend. I found that many women were seeking employment as cleaners through a lack of options and education. While these women play a critical role in our labour force, I was frustrated by their social confinement. I was also frustrated that people would use cleaning as a last resort of employment. I had myself a conundrum. I wanted to help these people, but I also wanted to inform the world that there is an art and a science to good cleaning, and we held the bar high.

One of the questions I ask every applicant in an interview is, "why do you want to be a cleaner, and why should we hire you?" It was during one of these interviews when an applicant described how she had been told by an abusive ex-partner that she felt she couldn't do anything else. I was moved to tears by her experiences, but at the same time inspired, wanting to help her and others like her to realise she had more potential than she gave herself credit for.

As my team began to grow, I was facing my own inner critic and would be riddled with self-doubt, questioning myself as a boss and a leader. It isn't in my nature to be unkind, so I thought I was weak because I wanted my employees to be happy and enjoy their work.

By now, I was in a relationship with a wonderful man, Scott, who held a leadership role in exploration drilling in the mining industry. I would tap into his knowledge and began modelling Clean and Cleaner on strict mining protocols, ensuring safety and procedures were our number one priority.

I started buying books and listening to podcasts based on leadership, assuming they would tell me all the secrets on how to "toughen up" to become a better boss. None of them did that. On the contrary, I was thrilled when I discovered that the personality traits I believed I already possessed: integrity, honesty, humility and empathy were all critical characteristics of a good leader. I'm far from perfect, but I became empowered by the knowledge I was on the right track. I could identify my own weaknesses, and I was obsessed with overcoming them, seeking help wherever I could.

In 2016 when I was 40 years old, Scott and I welcomed a beautiful baby girl into the world. Unable to clean in the final stages of my pregnancy, I started focusing more on the management and growth of Clean and Cleaner, and we won our first of many larger contracts, with baby in tow in her little car capsule as I visited new clients. In 2018 we became Clean and Cleaner Pty Ltd, which I was incredibly proud of.

I had a strong and capable team of cleaners, mostly women, and we remained small enough that I could get to know everyone. Through these relationships, I knew I wanted to help them. Despite representing over half the world's population, women lag behind men in property ownership, access to finance and education while traditional gender roles and expectations mean that many of them give up their dreams and careers because of their social situation.

Every single skill set I have used to run my business, I learned from the people who hired me, the people who trained me and those I worked alongside. I could write an entire book dedicated, in particular, to the remarkable women who helped light my path – the voices of impact with hearts of gold who, above all, approached everything with integrity. I wanted to pay it forward and share this light with these women, but with four children and a small business to run, I had very little time to focus on anything else.

My goal is to establish an environment where I can create security and opportunities for women of all ages through personal development and education. I'm still not sure how I'm going to achieve this, but I'm working on it.

For now, as I continue to raise my family and manage my business, I hope that simply by sharing my story, I can start helping and inspiring other women to overcome the challenges in their own lives. I have not suffered as so many around the world have suffered, but I have screamed, and I have cried, and I have felt pain. I have wanted to give up more than I care to admit, but the voice inside of me will always find a reason to get back up. I remind myself I am not finished, and I might never be finished, but I will always try to make a difference.

That's the principle that governs all things. In alchemy, it's called the Soul of the World. When you want something with all your heart, that's when you are closest to the Soul of the World. It's always a positive force.

~ Paulo Coelho - The Alchemist

About the Author

Colleen Dwyer is the founder and Managing Director of Clean and Cleaner Australia Pty Ltd. She is passionate about building her small business and creating pathways to assist other women to break free of social confinements and realise their true potential.

Since 2013, with Colleen at the helm, Clean and Cleaner has created employment opportunities for more than 60 people and inspired many to start their own cleaning businesses.

Colleen lives in Queensland with her partner, four children, one dog and two cats. She practices mindfulness, meditation and yoga daily and enjoys being creative with photography, video editing, writing and poetry. She also enjoys listening to music while gardening and cleaning the house.

Email: colleen@cleanandcleaner.com.au
LinkedIn: www.linkedin.com/in/colleen-dwyer4073
Website: www.cleanandcleaner.com.au

Voices of Impact

Jaime Lee Foord

What is your greatest memory? How do you relive that moment? Just through thought?

What if memories could be frozen in time? To relive them repeatedly as many times as you like.

This is my speciality, capturing moments in a keepsake to hold forever.

Hi, my name is Jaime Lee Foord. I am what I would like to think of as a mumpreneur. A woman of many skills and talents.

Empowering and mighty! Unfortunately, it didn't always feel that way.

Growing up as a child, it was still in an era where children were to be seen and not heard. This was cemented into my head for a very long time, creating what I assume are the building blocks of the foundation of the shy woman I became. Don't get me wrong; I certainly didn't have a horrible childhood growing up. But I was certainly carrying more baggage than I probably should have. I am a child of 4, the second eldest. 2 siblings of which have disabilities in some form. My mum would call me the angel child, I believe, because I was the only one to stay in line and do as they were told. I was moulded into it from a young age. I was helping other people before myself, helping my mum with my siblings and doing small chores around the house.

This was something I continued to do into adulthood, helping others before myself. A great quality to have is being empathetic, kind and generous. I always had hopes and dreams but never pursued anything, I guess deep down, believing I didn't deserve it anyway. I have always struggled with self-image and the way I thought about myself.

I left school at a young age, 16 to be exact, to start a hairdressing apprenticeship, it wasn't something I had wanted to do, but I was eager to get away from school.

Once I completed my apprenticeship four years later, I decided I wanted a real change away from everything I had ever known.

In some way, I guess I was running away from the life I had been living. But that is a story we aren't here to tell today.

I made my way to Western Australia to stay with my Aunty. That same week I started a new job, and I met my now Husband Dean through a mutual friend. Dean & I started only as a friendship and later into something more romantic. As our relationship grew, so did our lives, two years in, we found out we were pregnant with our first child Nate. At that time, I was halfway through studying for my diploma in Beauty Therapy, and Dean was working locally at a tyre shop.

The pregnancy was a large shock to us, as I had previously been told I might never have children due to having Poly Cystic Ovarian Syndrome. We were all very excited and, of course, nervous! We decided to make the move back to QLD so I could be closer to my own family during the transition into parenthood. Finding our first rental together in Nanango, QLD 2014.

Always having itchy feet, we found we moved around a lot, always looking for the next adventure. Yet, nothing truly felt like home.

Changing up every two years seems to be our thing. So we relocated again, residing in Rockhampton, QLD. That same year 2016, Dean & I were married at the local botanical gardens with our nearest and dearest.

Following our usual 2-year uphaul in 2018, we found ourselves pregnant for the second time; Dean had a new job opportunity, and we were relocating again. This time, we made our way inland to a small mining community called Blackwater.

Later in the year, Elijah was born, and at a time when there should be love and happiness, I did not feel that at all. Being so isolated in a small community away from family and friends.

I had developed post-natal depression. Things were very hard for me as an individual, as a woman, as a mother, a wife. Life, in general, had become unbearable, and I didn't know how to cope. I sorted out therapy and started taking medication to help. Both together certainly did and helped me move past some other things I had also been holding onto.

I had always loved photography but never pushed myself into

it. Wanting to do something for myself and get out of my comfort zone, following advice from my GP and therapist, I decided to study for a diploma in photography from home. It was a great option as I could study at my own pace from home while still being a hands-on mother.

Being told I couldn't do that or that I would never make something from it really drove me even more to do so. Just like a rebellious child, I did the complete opposite, of course.

I graduated with my diploma within six months and started my small business in the same year, 2019. The small community of Blackwater was fantastic in helping me with my business. In the small community feel, everyone knows everyone.

I made so many new friends, and connections and my confidence grew by the day, as did my new small business. And soon enough, I had actual paying clients wanting me to work with them! I was over the moon. I had so many opportunities to work with other local businesses and within the community, supporting the local football team and one of the local schools. In my first year of business, I was able to upgrade my camera equipment and enrol myself further into more photography education. But, the following year, Covid hit the world. Everything had stopped. I struggled as an individual and a business owner. But as a mother, it really hit home. We struggled to get assistance with our eldest son, who was later diagnosed with ASD and ADHD. So, for the sake of his health and wellbeing, we were once again on the move. We were relocating back to Rockhampton to seek the assistance we needed.

At a time when I thought I would never rebuild my business, it flourished! I grew to new heights as an individual and business owner.

And yet I still had my previous clients travelling from Blackwater to me specifically for photos. I had finally found my calling! I loved every moment of being a photographer and small business owner.

During this time, I met so many wonderful women who helped me on so many levels, especially when it came to my business and upscaling its potential.

I professionally and personally upscaled. I developed new skills I never thought I would need, let alone yet use. It was as though a chain reaction had gone off. The universe had listened, and it was finally providing me with the goods.

I started gaining awards and recognition and being published in global digital magazines, not just once but several times across many different brands.

The biggest contributor is Melanie Wood from Speaking Styles. Melanie has helped me find my voice and share my story. She has given me so much confidence in being myself and speaking my truth.

She has taught me so much, from her breath work, helping with anxiety and nerves, to confidence-boosting and getting myself in front of the camera, not just behind it.

I now have the biggest desire to help other like-minded women and families find themselves. This is because they recognise their beauty and let it shine through my photography.

I specialise in Maternity, Newborn and Family photography sessions. I am currently working through my certificates with the academy of newborn photography. This course is around the health and safety of newborns and mothers after birth. Each of my photography sessions is tailored around my client and what they hope to achieve from their session. I have worked with clients during pregnancy and then after the loss of their baby during birth. Creating something special and tailored to them and their situation.

During times of turmoil, photography can help so many people in so many ways. I honestly regret never having professional photos done earlier or more photos just from my phone during my time with post-natal depression, but at that time, it was the last thing on my mind.

I didn't have a single photo together with my youngest, Elijah as a newborn until he was a few weeks old. No one took a photo of me, just of the new baby or themselves with the new baby. It added salt to my pain, and I had an emotional breakdown about it one day, leading to at least one photo being taken of me with him. I don't love the image because I know the turmoil behind it. But it is all I have, so I still cherish it. Everyone's situation is different, and everyone deals with things differently. I am here to support you through it all with no judgement. It's always the mother/s taking photos of their babies and children or their loved ones. Never the other way around. This is still something I often struggle with now, more so because I am a professional photographer.

Here is your reminder, take those photos! Ask someone to take them! You are here, you are real, and you are worthy! Hire a professional. Make time for it and share some moments with your loved ones.

I have never heard someone say they regret having professional photos done. To capture special moments in one's life, there should be no regret. We may feel strong emotions around what we see in ourselves in the image, but the image itself means so much more.

Recently it has been another two years in our family's journey. My family and I have just relocated to the Peel region, Western Australia, home for my husband. His parents and sister live here and all his dearest friends. We sold up most of our belongings, only packing the essential items.

We packed up our car and drove across the country to get here. Although scary, exhausting and yet exciting, it has all been worth it. Starting all over again is just another speed bump in our journey, but we hope to be able to call this next chapter of ours a good one!

I have many massive goals, dreams, and desires for the not-so-distant future, especially owning my own studio space. To create a safe environment for women and their families to connect and feel their love. To capture their raw emotions and have these in keepsakes to cherish forever. I want to offer a personalised, luxury boutique experience like no other. I want to stand out from the crowd, have people see my work, and feel the raw emotions in each of my images. At the end of the day, we are all here for human connection and experience. I would love to learn more about videography also and be able to offer small video keepsakes with my current services.

I am always open to new adventures and trying new things! So, who knows what the next two years might manifest!

If there were one tip or advice you could take away from me today, it would be to book a photography session. It doesn't matter if it's just portraits of yourself, maybe with your partner or your much-loved pet.

Photos are priceless; without them, how are we to have these keepsake memories to look back on? To remember what someone looked like after they may have left this world. Time is precious, and so are you!

The best thing about a photograph is that it never changes, even when the people in it do!"

~ Andy Warhol

About the Author

Jaime Lee Foord is the founder/ owner of Jaime Lee Photography, specialising in maternity, newborn, and family photography sessions. Born and raised in sunny QLD Australia & currently residing on the beautiful western coast of Western Australia.

Jaime helps women and families create keepsake moments to look back on to remember the connection, emotion, and feelings from those moments. Featuring in global online magazines for her photography work. Jaime inspires to reach many people to create warm, heartfelt emotions from her images.

Jaime is an introverted, shy person who loves good coffee and cats! When she's not harassing the cat for cuddles, she spends quality time with her husband and two young boys.

Email: Contact@jaimeleephotography.com.au
Website: www.jaimeleephotography.com.au
Facebook: www.facebook.com/jaimelphotography

Voices of Impact

Dr Dee Hacking

'You are what you do, not what you say you'll do.'
~ Carl Jung

I feel like I am a participant in The Amazing Race, so I pop my backpack full of essential things and embark on a global race in competition with other players; I cannot see. In the pursuits and experiences, a fast-paced race for the finish line where one ultimately wins the grand prize. Mine is the amazing race of life, not a TV show for my 49 years on earth. I pick up my backpack of knowledge and personality and carry it with me daily, desiring something more out of each day, destined for great things and this amazing life with joyous experiences. I have come to know each exact moment of every day does not define us, but it does accumulate experiences to become the person we are today, with choice. I have always known from a young age I'm destined for something extraordinary. Have I made it yet?

Probably have, but each day I now know that *amazing* things happen when I do what I do best in my field of expertise. Assisting many but even just one person each day is very special to me and *IS* the most memorable thing anyone can do and ask for to be the giver of and recipient of too.

As I stand at the top of the stairwell, holding onto the handrail, looking over the railing of our new apartment complex to the floors below, the pretty contrasting patterns made by the descending bars, the stairs continue to make a fan pattern to then arrive at the base below. This exact image catapults me back to my 18 year-old-self, peering over the spiral staircase of my childhood home. The stairs with wrought iron rails were steep, each with a wide wedge at the periphery and a very narrow wedge at the centre of the spiral, not the easiest to traverse, and my father had tripped many times on them that I was assured to do the same. I felt clumsy each time I went near the stairs, as he did too.

"Clumsy movements lead to accidents" was a standard issue phrase. But, as I looked down from my lofty position, I saw patterns in the slate flooring below I had never noticed before; almond shapes and colour changes, and I decided I loved the slate. Mother had said she wasn't keen on the slate as it was icy in the winter and had miniature 'shelf-like tripping hazards' on the large slate tiles, so I had adopted the same opinion.

This memory then sends me back to an earlier time when we all lived in a unit, a complex of 12 ground floor units with a giant incinerator up the back, times when burning off rubbish was allowed. It was in the early '80s.

The long concrete driveway was perfect for me to rollerskate up and down, with many sharp dips and turns where the resident's garages pinched into the main driveway. After our trip to Fiji, I'd dance my rollerskates in tandem with a grass skirt and hula hoop manoeuvres. I was very multi-skilled, and the neighbours loved my driveway performances. My school friends would tell me it was a 'fancy front unit' years later. The crystal chandeliers glimmered in the lounge and dining room (Mother and I would take down crystal by crystal and polish, very hard to find a replacement crystal when I broke one, remember no eBay back then). The opulent living room had a grand light-filled Bay window and my bedroom with a garden view where I'd stare at the always blooming red and yellow climbing roses. Camelias with bird's nests, and baby birds with their demanding beaks and squeaks, watch the blue Wrens dart under the fallen Elm leaves.

On my first day of school, I stood in our private backyard courtyard space next to a potted Lemon tree growing in an old wine barrel, holding my brown briefcase *full of important things for my first day of school*. I felt the need to race off to school, so I didn't miss out on anything, not stand there for a photo; I *didn't have time for this!* I was also very keen to get home in the afternoons, so I didn't miss out on doing things Mother was doing. Looking back, I feel this moment set the tone for my life up until now.

Race, Race, Race. 'I haven't got time for this', zero patience, fear of missing out. True happiness is to enjoy the present, without anxious dependence upon the future

~ Seneca

Why do we all go through what we do in life? Many of my patients and regular clients also ask me this. My answer: Life experiences teach. We have our backpack of tricks within us to choose what we do with the rest of our lives. But, here lies the trick.

Do we let our past define us? I know many people with horrible, *horrendous* histories! Thank goodness I didn't. Do we talk ourselves into patterns that don't serve us well, or do we pay attention and design our own life, get out of it all, and create a life we want to live and thrive within, not simply exist? Precisely what we have done for ourselves, and now assist others to do the same. We have won our grand prize.

There is a spirit thief around. Yes! It's the real deal. I feel you want to know where it is too, as I have done for many years, and I shall tell you the exact location.

When I was a young girl living in the Garden Unit, I asked my father, "Why do I have to go through this?" After a bout of ear infections and being bullied on the school bus. His answer was, 'to teach you a lesson, young lady.' Now that may sound a little harsh, and I can feel you are thinking that too, but I had asked the same question at a different time to my Mother, Grandparents, and my Cousin, and they too all said a similar thing. "Listen to your body; it's teaching you things; life is teaching you!" A concept that is hard to grasp at a wee age. Hard to get even at a mature age. We all have it in us- the power to create- but first, Life experiences teach.

Why do we go through what we do in life; the ups-and-downs, the celebratory moments, moments of guilt and regret, and feelings of being unaccomplished?

Something I had asked myself just a few years ago.

'Why me?' It pops up when things aren't going so fabulously. *Why, why, why! I'm sick of it!*

THE TRICK: I no longer have an internal dialogue of 'why me'; the inner student of life that lives within me 'thanks herself for being her' within all the accumulated lessons, I do feel I am a voice of impact to others, healer to others, mentor and guide to others, how super amazing is that?

A peer of mine said only a couple of years ago, "you have the life everyone wants to live, do you know that? You look so blessed and lucky all the time!" and another colleague, "I wish I had your life!" and my Sister-In-law, "You're so lucky"!

"I'm no different from you", I reply; they don't believe me. I can see it in their eyes.

"It may look that way, but it doesn't feel that way to me; I work hard at it, but I'm just like everyone else where life gets in the way of a good plan, I feel guilt and shame just like everyone else, but I don't let it define me." I've found a way to be OK with it all.

Why do we believe our fears and guilts? It's the stories we tell ourselves and others. THE STORIES is where the Spirit Thief lies.

Operating from a space of impact without even knowing it:

A client of mine just last week came for her appointment at my Allied Health Clinic; we went through a few questions, and then she stopped the conversation. Then, instant tears running down her cheeks, she choked out, "Dee, you changed my life a few days ago!"

"Oh. Did I?" I hadn't seen this client for six weeks or so.

"A video clip you made came up on my feed," her whole body started to shake.

"You were explaining about designing your own life. Getting out of just surviving, and co-creating an exact life I desire to live, and the exact steps to do it, as you have done for yourself".

She confided in me that life's freight train had gotten away from her years ago and taken her on a ride of stress, ill health, emotional pain, and a life she didn't want to live (good things happened to her, but the remnants left didn't serve her well).

"I immediately started to do what you said, and my life has ALREADY changed. I'm going to show my husband tonight, and I'm so excited about our future now! So many things we want to create; the first thing is moving to a new home!"

Powerful. The client showed her husband, and they went to their financial advisor. Now they have a plan in place for buying a new home in another town, to travel around Australia in their Van and spend more time with their children and grandchildren and 'go out for coffee at a local cafe that they can walk to" (which they cannot to where they are currently living). All this from a 2-minute video of mine on her Facebook newsfeed.

My bag is *full of essential things,* life experiences, ups and downs, and impactful magical moments now coming to life for others.

My wonderful mentor and coach, Melanie, "pushed me" for over 12 months to expand out of my comfort and do these short live clips on my YouTube channel and Facebook pages. Impact to initiate new ideas, let others count on me and be my positive sparking self, as I AM ENOUGH.

I didn't believe her at the time, and I was so nervous I felt nauseated every time I went to go live; then I'd start and freeze, fear froze me, and I was mute. Finally, I started to become OK with how I was *feeling* and would do my funny 'out-takes' first, post, and then get serious. It turned out to be gold, and I connected on a different level with many people; many resonated with my' issue'.

It's time to give yourself undivided attention to concentrate on a good mood; it's all about the feelings you feel, the stories to tell, and the energy behind creation that brings you out of the pits of despair, even comfort zones, to clarity. It is taking back control of your inner self, planning out what you really desire, and stepping forth to design that for yourself.

BUT HOW is the burning question?

It's like when Pygmalion, the Greek King of Cyprus and

sculptor, wanted a wife so severely that he carved and chiselled out the perfect woman for himself in stone. Previously he had searched and searched, then realised there was no ideal woman for him. So he invented one himself from his inner desires. He fell in love with the statue he had carved for himself. He even went up to her and kissed her on the lips. To his SUPRISE, her lips felt warm. He looked at her lips were even pink. So he kissed her again, and the grey stone turned to real-life flesh, and she came to life.

In the same fashion, I, too, have designed the fantastic life I have created for myself. Then kissed life into it, yes though adversity, love, divorce, personal injury, highlights and low times too, It's actually relatively easy, and I can help you too.

I am a Doctor, Homeopathic Physician, Transformational Coach, Mentor, multiple business awards winner, and now an international bestseller Author. Living a blissfully happy married life with my gorgeous husband, John, the mother of three exceptional children, living on the beach, residing in our inner city apartment and running my Allied Health Clinical rooms and online Flip-Your-Life appointments assisting clients to become their best selves, continuing my authorship work too. Stumbling, purposefully (but not tripping upstairs or on slate tiles like years ago), through life, ticking one box at a time. Having many degrees and travelling to many countries, you can only imagine the 'stumbles' I've traversed, the hours of impatience, the *I'm so sick of this*, the *race, race, race*.

Isn't it empowering to know you do not need to 'master'

anything?

Life is awash with plenty; you can stumble your way through making more straightforward little changes in the direction you want to head, cultivating the FEELING like you are already there!

1. Design the life you want to live. Pay attention.

2. Your voice can impact others' journey through life.

3. Get excited. Speak up, even to yourself, and be mindful of your inner stories and voice and how it speaks to you.

4. Get out ahead of it all. Go that extra distance; you will be standing in the place of revelation, and more and more will come to fruition. It's about where you place your focus and the stories behind it.

5. *Operate from a space of impact without even knowing it.*

The path is right there, and there will always be more and more because that is flow!

Is it ever enough?

Of course, then more ideas come, and the path continues, these are those life experiences that teach, and magical things happen within blended clarity and alignment. Trust me. Attuning yourself to the current conditions you are in and bringing forth change, rather than hoping the requirements will change so you can be happy. Two very different things.

The magic. "If things were different, I'd feel better" Feel better first, and the situation will be different. Then, focus on a better feeling. Voila. Find a way to create the atmosphere of what you desire.

I knew this back at a younger age but didn't KNOW it.

My 'continued-ear-infection-and-burst-eardrum-self' figured out a way to never get ear infections again. My 'bullied-on-the-school-bus-self-decided to stand up for herself and became the new King-Pin of the bus, never to be bullied again.

What can I learn from this so it won't continue, and *how can I change this* to create what is best for me right now? In doing so, the energy of empowerment is an aligning force for you to co-create what you want to become. Life experience that teaches and, in turn, is impactful for others, for what do we want for ourselves and others other than to have a voice, be heard, be loved, and be joyous? I've learned to slow down, now more *rush rush rush, more patience, and no fear of missing out on anything*-there is plenty for all.

The spirit thief also lives on the other side of Enjoy The Process. Enjoy it, or you are cheating yourself. Most of us say, "NO! I want the result now; then I will enjoy the future". The spirit thief is your uncontrolled thoughts. You let your thoughts tell you a doomsday story or' a-sick-story', you tell others of all your horrendous problems, and your energy is awash with ground-zero-emergency feelings which is what you realise you now have more and more. The spirit thief is your thought processes and how you recognise this in your life experiences; what are you teaching others? Living daily inside your' most productive space' to turbocharge your momentum and enjoyment of your productivity, you have to combine the elements of doing more things you enjoy and setting yourself up for FEELING great about it all, and if not, BEING OK WITH IT.

'Before you heal someone, ask them if they are willing to give up the things that make them sick

~ Hippocrates

Dr Dee Hacking. Reach out, and I'd love to hear from you! www.drdee.biz

WHAT MY CLIENTS ARE SAYING:

"Dr Dee has changed my perspective. I want to get involved in the smaller details of my life and quit living on autopilot. Thank you for being inspirational, Dr Dee" - **Marco, Melbourne**

"I am telling EVERYONE about Dr Dee's practice. Any 'non-productive, non-self serving' conversation I'm in, I recommend it". - **Anita, Mackay**

Voices of Impact

"Amazing work you do, Dr Dee, in several areas, a REAL total care practitioner; I wish Dr Dee all the best in this lifetime and love her sparkling nature; it comes out in her work and her writing, and I can't wait for the next book she releases" - **Debbie, Melbourne.**

"Powerful and brilliant. This is just what I needed at this time of my life. I used to have dreams of a fulfilling life; I hadn't realised I had just given up. Life became busy and monotonous; I couldn't see a way out, so I just put up with it, as many people do. I thought this is life and it's as good as life gets...until now!"- **Robert W, Scotland.**

Wonderwoman Award 2021, Best Client Turn Around Award 2021- Entrepreneurial Business School, WIBBA Award nominee 2021, Stevie Awards Finalist Health Services Award 2021, Australian Rural Business Awards Finalist 2022, Woman In Business Award nomination 2022. International bestselling Author 2020 Change Makers and new release SPRUIK IT!-Cultivating the willingness to back yourself to success. Soon to be released, Aurelias Tide-paranormal fiction.

About the Author

Dr Dee Hacking has worked within the Personal Development, Medical, and Natural Medical industries for over 32 years while indulging in her passion for writing. She lives energetically towards her success for herself and her clients and has featured in medical publications for over ten years. Dee and her husband John currently provide Homeopathic services and Injury management, Transformational Mindset, Lifestyle, and coaching as successful Entrepreneurs in their businesses Living Lovingly, Bay Massage and Homeopathy Allied Health Clinics, and Hacking Enterprises company.

Dr Dee and John reside in Australia and the USA (John's home soil) and travel extensively, hosting workshops, live events, writing, and creating a lifestyle of their dreams with generosity and joy.

Email: drdee.homeopathy@gmail.com
Website: www.livinglovinglylifestyleflippers.com
Spruik IT Book: www.barnesandnoble.com/w/spruik-it-dr-dee-hacking/1142152553

Voices of Impact

Chrissy Harris

"Pets are so weird. It's just this little creature that lives in your house, and you can't speak to each other, but you're best friends."

I found this quote in a pack of motivational cards by Defamations Pty Ltd, and I share the sentiment that pets are more than our family: they are our best friends. That's why it's so painful when they leave our lives but never our hearts. My hope is to normalise conversations about grief after losing our best friends; in my story, it specifically relates to doggos. I want to share my journey of exploring creative outlets as a healing tool during my time of grief, with the intent of helping and supporting your transformation or someone you love.

I have often found common ground with colleagues, neighbours, friends, and even my gardeners, from our love of doggos by sharing anecdotes about the joy they bring to our days and how they express their cheeky personalities to brighten our days.

At the start of 2022, I had what I blissfully considered an ordinary life, sharing it with two large furbabes: a five-year-old Great Dane named Boss (his name is very misleading), and Molly, a seven-year-old Maremma Sheepdog. Molly had established herself as the top dog and dictated when Boss could, or could not, access his soft, comfy bed, the coolness of the hallway, or his favourite toy, which depending on the day, was either a palm frond, reindeer antler, soccer ball or a rubber tyre on a rope. They were in constant competition to be the first at anything: jumping in the car, jumping out of the car, running through the front gate or running down the stairs. Their days were full of simplistic competitions to ensure pack order was maintained.

We were guided by routine and rituals with many rigorously adhered to daily. Weekends included beach adventures, with every rock, seashell, and stick explored. The waves, however, were only of minor interest. Molly walked in as far as her chest, and Boss was barely in anything deeper than his ankles. Why? No idea! It's just who there were and what they liked.

One of my weekly rituals involved the removal of fluff from everywhere: floor, clothes, and vehicle air conditioner. It surprised me how the short hair from a Great Dane is just as much work as the long floof of a Maremma.

Playtime and training occurred at the same time every morning and afternoon, as though Molly and Boss could read a clock. If I had innocently lost track of time, I was kindly reminded of it when they both stood standing tall, staring intensely at me, with gentle excited panting in anticipation of the fun ahead. My agreement that playtime may commence was swiftly met with Molly and Boss running around the verandah and backyard sounding like a herd of elephants.

In their quiet moments, due to post-playtime exhaustion, I often enjoyed listening to their heavy breathing, which on occasion was accompanied by snoring at various volumes: from gentle whistles to thunderous wallpaper-stripping levels. A swift recording of the audio shared with my nieces would always end in contagious laughter. The distracting laughter would result in the doggos opening one eye to check on the excitement but most often deciding to return to their slumber.

Another weekend ritual was ordering coffee at a local drive-through café. Molly and Boss's large smiles would peer out the back windows, and they would receive more attention than me. 'I love your dogs!' most checkout operators would say as they waved hello and goodbye with a bright smile and a look of 'aren't you adorable!'

Between the two of them, Boss was the accident-prone one. The vets would welcome him with a keen interest in his most recent mishap and what it involved. By comparison, Molly was low maintenance with generally just a simple routine annual visit for vaccinations.

And what best friends don't like hanging out at the salon? Grooming was performed by local professionals with a remarkable set of skills; they can magically transform scruffy furballs into elegant creatures, including trimmed nails, coats smelling like your favourite ice cream flavour that you didn't know was your favourite, and sporting a new neck scarf embellished with their name. Boss loved his grooming so much that he once fell asleep resting on the shoulder of his groomer! The photos are still amongst my favourite captured moments.

This was my blissful life early in the year that I shared with Molly and Boss, but you know, sometimes life can take you on different paths with various choices, not all of them pleasant or easy to accept. This was the choice put before me. I discovered Boss had cancer, and all options provided a low quality of life. Consequently, this left me to make the hard choice of saying goodbye. A short four months later, with grief still lingering, Molly had both back legs permanently affected. Again, I faced options that involved a low quality of life. Again, my heart and mind fought to rationalise the choice to end her life was the kindest act for one of my best friends.

The grief of losing Boss and Molly unexpectedly was like a family member passing on each time. I assumed time and experience would get me through the loss of Molly, but I was facing different grief; it was compounded grief. No words could describe the depth of sadness. My heart was broken, and I was reduced to bouts of tears and snot bubbles. And lots of them.

When I first faced the loss of Boss, I didn't know how to process my grief. I found myself on a healing journey by creating my version of a funeral, exploring self-care and creative outlets, and seeking professional advice.

I spent hours online researching how to say goodbye in a way that would make sense of the emotional chaos I was experiencing. I found myself refusing to believe this was a final goodbye. I clung to the notion there was something deeper to experience. I explored with a strong sense of curiosity and a deep sense of awareness, and consequently, through unexpected experiences, I felt a sense of peace.

Fortunately for both Molly and Boss, I had a few days with them and was able to plan the final goodbye. This meant I could celebrate their final chapter here on earth by sharing our time and memories with our closest family and friends. Boss and Molly knew they were loved immensely and adored completely.

As the weeks cycled through the initial part of the healing process of each time, and I received a call each time to collect their ashes, I planned their funeral ceremonies just for me. I read sentimental poems and played celestial music as I spread their ashes in my garden, a place that holds many treasured memories. Throughout each ceremony, I felt a sense of knowing they remained with me, just in a different form.

To help process grief, I sought professional advice; consequently, I invested in self-care and explored stimulating and inspiring outlets. Coming from a creative background in a previous career, this process resonated deeply with me. It gave my mind something to focus on, and surprisingly I felt small but progressive moments of joy. Following are some of my healing processes, and I hope you will be inspired by at least one of these and explore what you or your loved one might need for a healing journey:

- Hammock: enjoy the thrill of being suspended in the air. Settle in with a good book, look up and cloud gaze or star gaze, or indulge in a nap

- Roller skating: hello, childhood memories!

- Gardening: I love to trim and shape my hedges by hand. It helps me to notice and appreciate and celebrate the delicate new growth

- Cooking: I learnt how to make focaccia bread with fine Italian flour, and I experimented with food art (inspiration found on Pinterest)

- Carving out time in the diary for self-care: every day, every week, every month

- Facing the feelings: invest in professional support (counselling and personal development)

- Taking a short period of leave from commitments: focus and work on processing grief.

Exploring what I needed to do to heal resulted in a deeper understanding of myself and others. If this is possible for me, it might just be possible for you also. Facing the challenges of grief and the loss of Boss and Molly, I was tested each time as I evolved and navigated my way through emotional triggers, adjusting to 'the new normal' and trying to understand unexpected spiritual experiences.

On one particular day, it challenged me more than on previous days to come home from work and walk by the empty food and water bowls; regular items that were once used to sustain my furbabes now felt obsolete and irrelevant. At that moment, I felt the emptiness, and so the tears flowed. Not wanting to throw away their bowls, I decided to simply relocate them to the storage cupboard, knowing that my friends and family visiting doggos could use these items on an ad-hoc basis. It was enough to give me a sense of ease at that moment.

As I returned to my weekly commitments, I knew there would be emotional triggers when my friends, family, colleagues and community members shared their condolences. Being an empath and wearing my heart openly on my sleeve, I knew I needed a plan to get through each day and remain professional and productive. As each beautiful soul shared their commiserations with me, I consciously chose to connect with their intent and genuine expression of love and care. I accepted their support with a heart full of gratitude that they cared enough about me and my experience to share their feelings. I repeat and draw your attention to one of my keywords for healing: gratitude.

Months have passed, and there are moments throughout each day when I think about Molly and Boss. Arriving home each afternoon, I am met with the silence their passing has created, so now I walk over to the boundary fence and give my neighbour's dog a scratch, which is always delightful for us.

Despite them not being here physically, I sometimes hear Molly and Boss's heavy feet running on the deck or their tails wagging and hitting the side of the house; I hear them as echoes in my soul, and in those moments, I consciously tune into feelings of love and gratitude for the memories.

Other times, I hear dogs barking in the neighbourhood, and I wait with anticipation that mine will soon join the choir while thinking, at least my dogs didn't start it this time! At an extended social outing, I can have the fleeting thought that I must go home and feed or walk the doggos. Routine, rituals, and muscle memories; takes time to reprogram. On the flip side, I don't need to vacuum quite as often because there is less doggo fur floating around (although it hasn't completely disappeared). Being a homebody, I admit that my social life has increased. However, I can no longer use the excuse that I can't come out because of #mydogs.

The spiritual experiences that followed Boss's passing were profound and unexpected. I felt a strong sense of his presence at home, and I saw his shape and form multiple times in various cloud formations. My favourite experience was cloud gazing from my hammock, and as I looked up, I saw his big happy face and large floppy ears formed in the clouds. He was looking down at me just as he did only a few weeks prior. Being a Great Dane meant we were head height whenever he leaned over the edge of the hammock to see what I was doing (no moment went unnoticed); thankfully, there was no drool this time.

One night, from the view of my bedroom window, I awoke to see the silhouette of Boss running in the treetops. In the timeframe between his passing and spreading his ashes, I noticed the fairy lights in the garden flashed differently, yet the settings hadn't been altered. I can't explain the 'why'. I can only share what I observed and felt. Every experience reminded me of his presence and love, which left me feeling a strong sense of peace.

My experiences with Molly passing were different. I desperately wanted to see her in the same way, but I couldn't force it. Instead, I had a visual impression each time I held my face to the sun and when I saw rainbows. In these warm moments, I saw her joyful face, and I felt at peace.

I have an Instagram page where I documented Molly and Boss and their big personalities and joyful moments. Although I no longer add new content to this page, you might enjoy reminiscing with me, @mollyfluff_itseverywhere

"From the greatest despair comes the greatest gift" is one of my favourite quotes from the video, 'The Secret', based on the book written by Rhonda Byrne. During my healing journey, this quote stood out for me and helped me focus on what I can bring to the world post-grief. The experiences have allowed conversations to evolve naturally at social gatherings; additionally, the self-care process has led me to regularly create fruit, floral, and frozen ice-related projects that I use to create joy for myself and others, including my Instagram community.

Friends have approached me and asked for advice on how I knew when the time was right for Molly and Boss to move on. I can only share from my own experience and encourage all owners to form an educated decision, including advice from their vet.

Other friends and colleagues have started a conversation, having heard about my loss, and openly shared their stories with me. I didn't know it at the time, but it has been in these exchanges that the healing continued at a deeper level.

I've learnt that grief is a personal journey, and the process and length of the healing time are different for everybody.

Bravely sharing my emotions and my understanding of reality with friends and family has provided space for the recovery process. I have felt comforted, heard, and understood. I have felt validated for what I experienced when others shared their own. Knowing that I'm not alone in navigating this journey is a relief, and neither are you.

These combined experiences have influenced my transformation. When I reflect on all the creative outlets that I explored, I can see the healing and how I was evolving.

The focaccia bread phase expanded as I explored food art by using various vegetables and edible flowers. My intrigue piqued, so I began freezing edible flowers in ice cubes, and soon after, I began to freeze flowers from my garden in ice cubes. This flicked a creative switch inside me, and I started making large ice coolers (for wine bottles and beverages at social gatherings), and in these ice sculptures, I froze flowers from my garden. I started to share these ice projects at dinners and small gatherings with friends and family. It became a challenging creative outlet for me, a talking point with my loved ones, and a shared admiration of something intriguing, completely unexpected, and oh so pretty.

I benefit from these frozen floral projects as it allows me to take a step away from grief and tap into my creative genius. I discover joy and wonder in experimenting with each new ice project. Did you know? When exposed to the low temperature in the freezer, some flowers get ice burn; but some don't.

I thrive on being the designer and creator of projects I can share with my loved ones. It starts with the first reveal, followed by the heightened curiosity of observing the melting process. It takes hours for the large ice coolers to melt, and as it melts, flower petals and leaves reveal themselves as an evolving art form, creating a 3D effect. It is an object of delight admired for hours and enjoyed by everyone, making a beautiful, shared memory.

The more I invested in conversations, creating floral and frozen projects and sharing memories, somehow, over time, the overwhelming grief and sadness eased. And with a heart full of peace, my healing process gets easier as I continue to feel gratitude for the time I had with Molly and Boss and for their impact on my life, both then and now.

This is a short introduction, and I would love to be able to share more of my story on a podcast. If you would like to hear more or feel it could potentially help your audience, please send a DM via my Instagram page, @floralandfrozen

I continue to embrace opportunities to share stories and normalise conversations about grief from losing our pets - our best friends - and I delve into various projects as outlets for caring and nurturing myself.

A hobby has evolved from what started as a channel to direct my grief, and I enjoy sharing photos and time-lapse videos with my loved ones and the Instagram community. I have no idea where this will go just yet, and perhaps it could end up being something greater, but for now, I continue to use the journey to share my artistic gifts born out of despair, as the quote says.

By sharing my story, my hope is to showcase what has been possible for me, and my wish for you is that you're able to find peace and gratitude in your healing journey or for a loved one in your life that might be going through this process.

About the Author

Chrissy Harris is a visionary and creator of work that inspires and enhances awe, wonder, mystery and intrigue. Her formal career and community engagement started with her own photography business and has developed further now working in Community Relations and Human Resources for a large local company. Over the years, Chrissy has helped, supported, and inspired her dog owner community to share their stories to make a difference in growing as confident dog owners and, more recently, processing loss and grief. Chrissy enjoys learning about human and canine behaviour and nurturing her numerous indoor and outdoor plants. While walking on the beach, Chrissy will often meet new doggy friends; she also enjoys travelling and socialising with family and friends while watching the sunset over the iconic Gladstone region in Queensland.

Instagram: www.instagram.com/floralandfrozen

Voices of Impact

Donna Kirkland

It's Not Over...

There embedded within every story, there exist even more stories, each one interconnecting, leading into the account presently told. It is an infinite conversation from the beginning of time to all eternity. Each of us is a part of a larger story, our lives somehow intertwined without us even knowing. You see, we are on a different journey, yet we are on the same path. We are born... and we die. What unfolds in the middle reveals our identity, or rather The Who or What we place our identity in.

There are many stories within my journey; I have overcome physical and sexual abuse, seasons of poverty, alcoholism, cancer, attempts at suicide and more ... and yet. Yet, what pulled me through each storm was one familiar, still, small voice gently guiding me through the dark.

There has never been a promise that life would be without trials. However, we do have promises. One of the most significant promises we can hold onto is that our God, our Creator, loves us and that HE will never leave us nor forsake us. Unfortunately, we often try to determine what that love looks like and don't trust the loving God. We scream out, asking where HE is amid our pain - I've done this, and I'm sure you have too. HE is always there. Sometimes we just aren't listening, or we aren't listening with the right heart.

I remember the deep valley of depression I fell into following the passing of a beautiful friend who had lost her battle with cancer.

I was totally empty, without words, furious that my God could let this happen to the most wonderful, faith-filled, spiritual woman I knew. Yet, believing with everything in me that the blood Jesus shed at Calvary was enough, I had trusted that she would recover.

How, then, could I honestly and with conviction continue to proclaim that Jesus loves, Jesus saves, and Jesus heals??? … my faith was truly being tested…

***

What is the anchor in your life that keeps you grounded, calm and steady with just a glimmer of hope when everything seems to be going wrong?

My anchor is God's still, small voice, only recognisable via a living relationship with His son Jesus Christ. Looking back over many years, I can now clearly identify significant junctions in my life journey, at times when I felt most alone, where HE showed up in the person of His Holy Spirit. These were pivotal moments within the seasons of my pilgrimage that carved out who I am today.

One such instance was back in the late 70s. It was a Saturday evening, and I was excited to be away from my small hometown, attending a combined church's Easter Camp Weekend. I was at the rear of a long hall filled with excited teenagers. Most of us were not there for the right reasons. For me, it was just an opportunity to get away from home. I was standing in response to a stirring in my heart that arose when the young speaker down the front extended an invitation to pray with him. I don't exactly recall what I prayed, nor can I confess that I felt differently- however, I can testify that my life truly began to change following this vocal affirmation. It would be many years before I revisited this prayer with any understanding of its significance to me or its relevance that day.....

***

My young life quickly racked up a scorecard of failed relationships, each one leaving its battle scars. One such relationship had provided an avenue of escape from the small dead-end town where I grew up. He drove me away from the painful experiences of home. With him, a new story unfolded in a new coastal town some 300km from where I had first begun...

I was seeking a job and seated opposite a gentle, kind little lady in an empty restaurant room on the second floor of the local serviceman's club. "I am sorry, but I don't have any jobs for you right now, dear"; she paused, then proceeded to write her name and phone number onto a piece of paper. Finally, she passed me across the table with instructions to place it into my purse and leave it there until I needed it.

I had thought this odd at the time. Still, nonetheless, I was obedient to her voice. I walked away without thinking again of the small slip of paper tucked safely inside my wallet.

Time passed, and things started going very wrong with this new boyfriend. He had revealed his bisexuality and drug use and was violently possessive. I had decided to get out of the relationship 'whilst the getting was good, so to speak. As I ran down the house stairs that day, I glanced back over my shoulder; my eyes were drawn to the large butcher's knife he gripped as he chased me down, screaming, "You can't leave; I will kill you first!".

I had already packed my entire life into my little Mazda 1300, and I managed to get away, though coming up fast in my rear-view mirror was my now absolutely ex-boyfriend, hot in pursuit driving his souped-up Ford Falcon... a voice in my head... "the note!" I pulled up at the first telephone booth with a screech (we didn't have mobile phones back then) and squeezed inside through the glass doors, pulling out the tiny piece of paper with a name and number from the back of my purse. I dialled the number, and a calm woman answered... "Hello Donna, is that you? I have already prepared your bed and room; come now quickly." She had given me the address, and my ex was bashing on the phone booth walls, knife in hand. I don't recall just HOW I got past him, but I made it again to my car and sped away towards sanctuary and safety.

As I drove hastily into the foreign garage at the address I had been given; the gentle, kind woman swiftly pulled the roller door down behind me. Just in the nick of time, I was evading the Falcon that noisily prowled back and forth along the street, unsuccessfully searching for a lead as to where I had disappeared.

That night, as I sat in a shallow bath, shell-shocked from all that had transpired earlier, I cried out to God, tears streaming down my face. Then, a warmth came over me, and a new language flowed from my lips - it was the weirdest thing... I couldn't understand what I was speaking, but it filled me with strength, courage, and peace. Later that evening, I asked the woman what she thought it may have been, but she replied, "It's time for bed, dear. Tomorrow, we will take you to Armidale, where I have arranged an interview for you to get into university."

Looking back on this incident, I recognise how God intervened on my behalf and protected me. I am encouraged by the Bible verse, *"keep on loving each other as brothers. Do not forget to entertain strangers, for by so doing some have entertained angels without knowing it"*(Hebrews 13.2 NIV). Even though she was the one extending love to a stranger, I have never been able to find this gentle woman since she set my life back onto the right course.

***

I had unfortunately not learnt from my mistakes nor remembered the blessings that had resulted in my new life course. So instead, I managed to continue the same self-destructive path, out of control, channelled along by wrong choices in men and life in general.

About two years had passed, and I was now a uni dropout. I

found myself in yet another new town. While working at a service station roadhouse and lost after removing myself from a violent relationship, I stopped for a work break. I prayed a short prayer under my breath. What followed was a familiar yet still unknown language bubbling out over my lips, the same as once before, almost two years previously. That sense of peace now comforted me, though I had no idea what it was. Looking at the tall, dark stranger now seated in the roadhouse restaurant, I reflected on the previous months…

My recent partner suffered from diabetes and struggled to manage his illness to the degree that hypoglycaemic reactions and an extremely low blood sugar level were common. He was an out-of-control rum drinker who never knew when to stop and refused to take his lifelong illness seriously. He would neglect proper eating and expect me to mop up his messes in life and health alike. The outworking of these low blood sugar reactions, "hypo's", would often end in violent physical outbursts, and I was usually the victim. Tormented on a regular basis to the point where I could no longer discern between "hypo" and pretend "hypo", I felt trapped. I felt a confusing sense of duty towards his health, versing the fear of the gun he kept under the bed, "in case you should ever try to leave me," he had said. I can remember bashing my forehead against a brick wall out of desperation, trying to knock myself out, somehow escaping the mental anguish of it all.

One day during a "hypo", my fiancé - yes! I had accepted a marriage proposal; can you believe it? - was deteriorating into a comatose state. A briefing from his mother had armed me with knowledge of what to do in such an emergency, which required an injection. It should have been into the vein, though I had injected it into his arm muscle in my haste. I made a quick phone call to our family doctor, who immediately arranged an ambulance. The doctor arrived ahead of the ambulance and sat beside my fiancé, reassuring me my injection mistake was harmless. It merely meant the contents would take longer to enter his system and would result only in a sore arm muscle. My fiancé, regaining consciousness, came up swinging, smacking the Dr across the jaw! That moment would change the direction of my life as the Dr turned to me and barked, "Does he do this always?". I shyly nodded. I heard the words that came next loud and clear as my Dr said, "You need to pack your things and leave this man today! You do NOT have to put up with this."

That evening I walked into the hospital, post visiting hours, with my fiancé's exceptionally crisp, freshly ironed pyjamas. I burst into the shared wardroom with bold resolve and threw the pyjamas at him. Announcing our engagement was off – and I never wanted to see him again- I declared, "I deserve better than this!".

For several months after, I had taken refuge with a female work colleague. But then, I heard that my new ex had left town and returned to his family. His sister once visited, begging me to reconcile, but I had tasted what my life with him would look like, and I made it clear that that life was not for me.

My then flatmate was moving on, leaving me to fill her spot to afford the rent. I was living in a fabulous space above a shop in the historic central business district, and I loved it. However, there was no desire to relocate, so consequently, I had chosen to advertise for a flatmate, and a considerable period had passed with zero response. I was desperate when at last, a call had come.

That sole applicant was now sitting in the Roadhouse restaurant where I worked. I believe peace and strength were drawn from the strange language flowing out of the somewhat blasé prayers. I had prayed that emboldened my decision to accept the handsome dark-haired stranger's application, relieved at no longer having to foot the rent bill on my own.

Later that evening, when I returned home, the answering machine was loaded with numerous offers to share rent. Where had they all come from, and why now, after I had already given the keys and lease to the dark-haired stranger?

Looking back, I cannot believe this little story and the sequence of events that followed. Although it could, have been a mere coincidence in life, that same man, some years later, became my husband of now 31 years.

Life with my husband has been one of a blended family, and the "days of our lives dramas" are commonly synonymous with that. We have, between us, six children and 16 grandchildren thus far. Yet, within our marriage story exists layers of experiences, struggles, battles, losses, and victories ... all with one common denominator... One that has continued to journey with me, alongside me, but more often, carrying me, my God - even before

I knew Him.

My journey includes everything from a professional national and overseas singing career to mission trips in multiple countries around the world. Along with my husband, I own and have managed multiple businesses and am currently an elected Local Government Councillor. Our lives are creating a book of family stories that my children will share for generations to come. You see, life's twists and turns led me first, and later my husband, into a glorious promise-filled relationship with Jesus. I came to learn the language of the Holy Spirit and how He has guided me over the years.

Scripture in the 78th psalm teaches that we should share those stories, not hide the truth, preventing our children from repeating the mistakes of the generations that went before them. They instead can set their hope anew on God, remembering His glorious miracles and obeying His direction for their own lives.

The Holy Spirit of God alone can make us what we ought to be, and it is our faith in the finished work of Jesus Christ at Calvary that sets the parameters for how far we will grow and develop.

By knowing Him, our lives take shape; He lives in and through us. *"This is how we know we're living steadily and deeply in Him, and He in us: He's given us life from His life, from His very own Spirit. Also, we've seen for ourselves and continue to state openly that the Father sent His Son as Saviour of the world. Everyone who confesses that Jesus is God's Son participates continuously in an intimate relationship with God. We know it so well; we've embraced it heart and soul, this love that comes from God."* (1 John 4:13 the Message Bible)

***

So how did I end up reconciling the loss of my dear friend mentioned at the beginning of this chapter, and how did I restore my faith?

That still, small voice wrapped around me and spoke gently. HE reminded me of a time when my eldest born was throwing a mighty tantrum... writhing and thrashing about on the floor, lamenting, "why can't I have it! I want it now!"... or words to that effect. He was livid with me as his mother for not delivering what he had wanted at that time. I sat on the floor next to him and pulled him tightly, wrapping my arms and legs around him, protecting him from hurting himself until he calmed down. I just held him and didn't speak until I felt the energy fall away, his breathing calm and rhythmic, not chaotic and frantic as it had been before. At that point, I whispered, "I am your mother, I love you, and only do what is right for you; you cannot have what you asked for simply because 'I say so". To try and explain the reasons validating my decision would have been wasted breath on the young boy who lacked wisdom for the truth. I knew what I was doing, and that mattered; he would have to accept it.

The Holy Spirit used this memory to teach me that God is sovereign, and as my son had thrown his tantrum, I had been doing with my Father God. God was holding me safely, waiting for me to calm down so that I could hear when He spoke... listen to Him as He said, "Because I am God, and because I love you

Donna... it is what it is, because I say so." I would never know why my friend had not been healed.

I realised then that I had put God into a box of what I thought He looked like and how I thought He should behave - I had forgotten WHO He was and all that He had already done for me.

My heart softened that day as I relaxed into His arms, safe knowing that He never leaves nor forsakes me.

Knowing that I can turn to Jesus for anything, anytime, anywhere has set the foundation for me to see miracle upon miracle; each one is a story in itself. My husband was healed of epilepsy; my youngest daughter was healed of a life-threatening condition; relationships were restored, and financial miracles. Overseas I prayed in faith and saw a child healed of tuberculosis, women conceived who previously could not, and souls set free from the torments of life's issues.

My story is still unfolding; as a multiple business owner and currently an elected Local Government Councillor, I choose with my heart to listen to him daily. So that I might be ready to hear whenever His still, small voice speaks... leading me along His path and out of the valleys I walk through.

Don't be afraid to take that leap of faith and ask HIM for help; invite HIM into your world.

For You: Read Romans 8:5-17

FOR US: IT'S NOT OVER ...

About the Author

It has been said, "Donna is the kind of person that people aspire to be". Passionate and perseverant, she is a recognised public figure in the City of Rockhampton, known for her community work, advocacy, brilliant communication skills, vibrant personality, generosity, and honesty. Her resume encompasses everything from leading recovery groups to spending years as a Women's Community Projects Coordinator; mentoring women's ministries in Ukraine; creating Charity Family Fun Days (raising more than $100,000); owning and managing multiple businesses simultaneously while raising children and grandchildren.

She is a founding member of 'The Shelter Collective' (fundraising organisation for affordable housing solutions), and now serving her wider community as a Rockhampton Region Local Government Councillor. Donna dreams big and is unphased by life's stumbling blocks.

Email: Donna4Rocky@gmail.com
Facebook: facebook.com/DonnaMKirkland
LinkedIn: linkedin.com/in/donnakirkland

Faye Lawrence

'How the fuck did my life come to this?' The question reverberated around my head like a spectacularly pernicious tormentor. Bleary-eyed, nauseous and with head thumping, shame-filled tears flowed profusely down my face. I was being admitted to the hospital's inpatient detox unit, a fact I was still trying to get to grips with.

The humiliation was brutal. Being the eldest of four kids born in the 70s, I had always pictured myself as the one who held it together and helped everyone else. The one in charge. I despised the pathetic weakness of drinking in the family home, my blood boiling at the empty bottles found hidden in bedroom drawers and dramatic scenes. Alcohol had left generational imprints on both sides of my family. And yet, despite all that, here I was. I made a vow to myself there and then; I would never come back here again.

Ten days earlier, my eldest daughter had brought me to the emergency department in an extremely inebriated and highly distressed state. My mental health was fine, I insisted to the psychologist; then, it was the alcohol that was making me want to throw myself off my fifth-floor balcony. There were no beds available, they said, and an admission date was scheduled.

Secretly, I was relieved. While I did desperately want help, this reprieve meant the party wasn't over just yet. I had ten whole days to get used to the idea of a proper goodbye to my beloved booze. Like a surreptitious farewell fling with an illicit lover, you know you ultimately must leave; this meant I could fully immerse myself in drinking now, all day and all night.

What had started out as a fun, social and cultural rite of passage some 30 years earlier had descended into the pit of despair, hopelessness - and days spent strategically alternating bottle shops - I was in now. There was absolutely nothing fun about this anymore.

High-functioning problem drinkers are often exceptionally adept at keeping all the balls of their life in the air (just about) so that even at this stage, friends had little idea of how bad things really were behind closed doors. As a society, we perpetuate this false narrative that drinking is not a problem until you've lost it all, and, based on that, I was still 'fine'.

I was incredulous, almost admitting that things had become this bad, that I was not in control of my drinking. God knows I'd tried enough times. But me? I mean, I had a career, a degree, a nice car, and I drank Pol Roger; people like me didn't need a detox. Except that they did, and they do.

And the reality was I just couldn't push down my deep sadness and unhealed trauma with alcohol anymore, no matter how hard I tried. There had grown a gaping, dark void inside of me that no amount of alcohol could satiate anymore, and frankly, it terrified me.

Now, with my last hurrah done and dusted, I was in hospital admissions blowing into a breathalyser before most people had had their morning coffee. They say the truth will set you free, and it did. Admitting I couldn't do this alone made it real to me more than anyone.

The detox unit was a separate stand-alone part of the hospital. The door slammed and locked behind us. You were free to leave whenever you wanted, I was told, but that signalled you'd forfeit your place. There were no phones, devices, internet, visitors, or cigarettes. I had been lucky to get in at all. There were only 16 public beds for both drug and alcohol detox in a state of over 5 million people. Because, well, no one really gives a shit about addicts. They bring it on themselves. To be fair, it's pretty much what I thought until I was one.

Detox isn't rehab; it's where you go to medically withdraw from your drug of choice before either going back home or going on to rehab. It is usually located within a hospital because of the risk of seizures mainly, so patients can be transferred quickly to the correct specialists.

Rehab wasn't an option. No one really knew I was here, and I fretted about what was I going to tell work if I had more time off. I just needed this, needed something, now. I'd worry about the rest of it later.

I decided to brave it and venture down the corridor to the common room to mingle with the other patients, not knowing what to expect. There was a whiteboard at the front of the room with words half smudged out. It had an ancient TV mounted up on the wall, and orange pleather chairs with wooden arms adorned the periphery. In the middle was an assortment of well-worn magazines and what looked to be some old games and puzzles with the obligatory pieces missing.

I mumbled an awkward 'hey' to the other patients, woefully ill-equipped for the social niceties in these kinds of situations. At that moment, I felt like a bit of an imposter. Was I even addict-y enough to be here? Maybe drinking red wine for breakfast didn't warrant a bed here after all.

Over the course of the next six days, I was going to get an education that money could not buy. I was going to bond with the others and hear their stories – among them, a policewoman, a bikie, a teacher, an ophthalmologist, a chef, a sex worker, an unemployed muso I fondly called Tom Hardy – and I was going to humbly learn that addiction is a great leveller. It doesn't discriminate. In here it didn't matter what your job, socioeconomic status or your education was. We were all ultimately there for the same reason.

How it started

There are some moments that are so utterly life-changing that they are seared into your brain forever. I can only describe the sense of relief the first time I got really, really drunk as one of those; it just turned my brain off. Finally, I had some respite from my incessant, swirling thoughts. I was about 13.

"This isn't lemonade," I said to my cousin, up in the kid's bedroom at my grandparent's place, where we would hang out while the grown-ups were downstairs getting drunk. "Yes, it is", he said. It wasn't, but I didn't care, and I kept drinking them, one after another. At last, I'd found the answer. I could escape being me.

Later that afternoon, I was dragged out along the pavement, disgraced, and thrown into the back of the car, where I promptly vomited for most of the hour-long journey home. There began decades of largely unhealthy alcohol use.

Like many, I had the rite-of-passage-in-the-UK teenage stuff of partying too hard, clubbing, experimenting with drugs, and being a trash bag, but things were really going to ramp up for me in my early 20s. My ever-present anxiety was now off the charts. I was having panic attacks regularly and would drive to shops over the other side of town just to avoid bumping into anyone I knew.

Alcohol was the only thing that made me feel ok. I started drinking earlier and earlier to get some respite from what felt like constant terror at just being alive. Fast forward a few years, and I was living in Australia and soon to be a newly single parent with no support network, having only been in the country for a year.

By now, I was struggling to stay afloat. Juggling two very young children, working and commuting, a house and yard to keep, my terrible anxiety, plus the emotional and financial impact of a marriage breakdown, was a lot. I was so alone.

I didn't have the children on the weekends, and I would completely obliterate myself – anything I could get my hands on to escape the load I was carrying. Things were getting out of hand, fast. It was late 2001, and after seeking help from my GP, I started alcohol counselling and was put on naltrexone. There was no way I wanted to stop, but I knew I needed to rein it in. In what I retrospectively consider to be a sliding doors moment, the amazing counsellor I'd been having success with left the practice, and his replacement told me after a couple of sessions that I didn't have a problem after all. Well, when the professionals tell you you don't, then I guess you don't. Years later, I know from others how horribly common that experience is.

Over the period 2001-2017, I sought help on and off. AA, alcohol counselling, GP, Campral, more Naltrexone, books on how to stop drinking, psychologists, and online supports. But none of it would stick.

There were many, many incidents over this time that were outrageous, dangerous, and toe-curlingly mortifying. The time my two front teeth were knocked out after a drunken piggyback and hitting the pavement with my face. At the time, I could not find my keys in my bag, so I passed out on my front lawn, only waking as the neighbours were going about their day. The time a cab driver turned up on my doorstep demanding payment as I'd refused to pay him the night before, after a drunken argument, I hadn't even remembered. The many times I had woken up with randoms or people I didn't want in my bed. So many stories I would, even now, be too embarrassed to share.

Often – maybe thankfully – I would not be able to fully piece the evening together without retracing my steps through texts, phone calls, bank statements and tentative messages to friends. That dreaded feeling of knowing you had done something, but you couldn't quite remember what or who you needed to apologise to, was all too familiar. On the back of any particularly regrettable incidents, I would swear off the booze. Enough was enough, I'd think; this isn't the person I want to be. But by the weekend, I was always back to square one.

Despite all this, I would be lying if I said there weren't many fun times in there, too. I loved nothing more than getting frocked up to go out on the town and the decadence of fine dining. The anticipation of the night ahead. The freedom of it all. A couple of glasses while getting ready. Food and wine matching. The nights out with girlfriends flitting about from bar to bar, giggling and flirting. Nipping out for a cigarette and becoming besties with people you didn't know. Wiling away sunny Sunday afternoons in the beer garden. But the missing ingredient was moderation; if I could just master that, everything would be fine.

Sometimes I would successfully make changes for a while. I'd carefully note the number of units I was drinking a day. I would stay away from wine and only drink vodka, lime and soda. I would say I was only going to drink from Thursday to Sunday. I'd start a Febfast (failing thrice). I would try and set limits on the number of drinks I'd have when I went out. It never lasted.

During much of the time I was drinking problematically, I was also doing pretty ok in life, and this is where the cognitive dissonance really bites. I was holding down a demanding job, studying, raising my children, working out and doing all the adulty things. But the nature of alcohol use disorder is that it's progressive. And it was only a matter of time before the wheels well and truly fell off.

How it's going

When I left detox in late 2017, I knew things would have to be different this time because I feared I wouldn't make it if I went back to drinking. A radical shift in mindset and lifestyle was going to be needed. So, I set about doing whatever it took – changing up my routines, therapy, alcohol counselling, medication, online communities, some AA and ACOA stuff, in the beginning, saying no to things, staying home when I needed to, getting out when I needed to.

When you've spent your whole adult life with drinking firmly at the centre of your identity, finding out who you are without is bewildering and terrifying. I was the party girl, the life and soul; that's who I was, who I'd always been. I felt I was letting people down if I wasn't those things. I had no idea how I was going to fit anywhere or whether people would still like me; now, I didn't drink. I also had zero clue about how to deal with my feelings without alcohol.

This is usually where people give up on sobriety for two reasons:

(1) peer pressure from others or feeling socially excluded, and (2) learning to sit with uncomfortable feelings, often without any skills to equip them to do so. Neither of these things is easy to navigate.

Quite quickly, I started to realise I was gaining a lot – my health, my sleep, my finances, my skin, my weight, my clarity, and my relationship with my kids. Most of all, though, was my relationship with myself. I started to have my own back. I was becoming reliable instead of breaking my promises over and over. I started to treat myself better, challenging the harsh inner critic that was continually pulling me down and berating me. I started to believe I was worth something. I was walking my talk, and as a result, I was becoming proud of myself. These were things I had been looking for my whole life. It was like a revelation to me! Why on earth had I waited until I was 44 to do this?

There were unquestionably many challenging, incredibly difficult and uncomfortable moments, but none of those could outweigh the monumental growth I was experiencing.

After about a year, I decided I wanted to branch out a bit with my social life, but I didn't want to be around people who were drinking heavily. I figured there must be lots of other people like me, people who didn't want to drink or couldn't drink but who still wanted to have an active social life. I looked but couldn't find anything.

So, in late 2018, I decided to start up a MeetUp group called

Untoxicated (Booze-Free Fun and Friendship) in Brisbane, which was exactly that. Numbers grew, and I soon opened a group in Sydney with a friend helping to host events and an online support community.

Then, in June 2019, ABC's 730 Report produced a segment on Untoxicated – what we were about, why we started and my story. Baring my truth on national TV was pretty scary stuff, a dirty secret, being aired in public. I honestly feared I would never work again.

Still, I decided that if we were to start breaking the stigma around not just problematic alcohol use but shifting the negative narrative about being sober, then stories like mine had to be shared. After all, 1 in 4 Australians are impacted by an alcohol, drug or gambling problem, so it's not exactly unusual. It seemed utterly nonsensical to me that something that touched so many should be hidden away. From what I could see, that just stopped people from reaching for help when they needed it.

Things really took off after the 730 Report. We opened another group in Melbourne, and soon, we had thousands upon thousands of members. It was incredible to see how many people were engaged with Untoxicated. Our hosts were all volunteers who had lived experience and wanted to give back. Members didn't have to be sober 24/7, just at the event. This meant they could 'dip their toes in' and come along and give it a try and meet others who were just like them.

We wanted to show that life with less or no alcohol could be fun and enjoyable, which meant that people came for a raft of different reasons – cultural, religious, wellness – and attending didn't automatically indicate problem drinking. Lots of people wanted to socialise without alcohol; movies, dinners, camping, karaoke, roller discos – we did it all!

Untoxicated evolved into the largest alcohol-free social community in Australia and a volunteer-run health promotion charity helping its 10,000 members forge new sober connections and supporting changes to their drinking habits.

In the process, my life has changed immeasurably. I became a TED speaker, made many media appearances, speaking at conferences, and now practice as a sober coach. Using my psychology degree, coach training and continuing study in post-grad counselling, I have been privileged to support hundreds of people to change their relationship with alcohol over the last 5 years – whether that's been through coaching, informal support, advocacy, or through my work with Untoxicated.

I have endeavoured to make my mess my message, to help others realise they are not alone, that they can have a full and rewarding life without alcohol, and to know that they are not a terrible person for the ways they have tried to deal with their pain. They are just like me, just like you, just like all of us – fallible human beings - and they deserve compassion and support.

I have also learnt there is much to be gained by being vulnerable and in owning your story. When you bring the darkness into the light, you take your power back. More than that, you are paving the way for others to do the same, showing they can unburden themselves from the weight of shame too.

As it turns out, my experience of being in detox - which was the lowest point in my life - was my most empowering and liberating. It became the springboard to a new life I could never have imagined. I am forever grateful to the people who helped me along the way.

And just like I promised myself, I never ever did go back there again.

About the Author

Having been a heavy but high-functioning drinker since her teens, Faye Lawrence wound up in inpatient detox in late 2017 after the wheels really fell off. Determined not to let her sobriety ruin her social life, she started Untoxicated, which grew into Australia's largest alcohol-free social community with over 10,000 members. Faye is a TEDx speaker and has featured on 730 Report, ABC News, Business Insider, Prevention Magazine and many more. A social butterfly and a bit of an idealist, she believes in a world where everyone belongs and advocates to normalise sobriety and reduce the stigma around addiction.

Faye's lifelong fascination with human behaviour led her to complete a psychology degree and further study in post-grad counselling. She is now a Grey Area Drinking Coach, partnering with people to make changes in their relationship with alcohol and live happier, more fulfilling lives.

Email: faye@untoxicated.com.au
Website: www.fayelawrence.com.au
Instagram: www.instagram.com/_fayelawrence_

Voices of Impact

Christine Lennon

Winston Churchill once said Pessimists see challenges in every - opportunity while optimists see opportunities in every challenge. Throughout my life, I have tried to be an optimist, finding a positive in every situation.

Often, we can't see our own potential, and it takes someone else to assist us to see that. I am extremely grateful for the people in my life who have helped me to find mine.

When I was 10 years old, I was very fortunate to have a teacher who was the first person in my life who made me realise that I could do anything I set my mind to. He also helped me to find my voice. Not that I wasn't already a confident child, but it was the start of my love of speaking. It was when I consciously started to not be restricted by boundaries and when I was told that I couldn't do something, I set about proving I could.

Several years later, I was working for my sister's partner in his business. I was a 'Girl Friday' all sorts of administration work which included being a receptionist, invoicing, debt collecting, making morning and afternoon teas for the mechanics in the business, banking, and cleaning cars. When the car salesman left, I said I could do his job, and my boss agreed. Now I don't know why he agreed to let me do it, it may have been that he was my sister's partner, but I am grateful to him for doing that. I am eternally grateful to the people I had in my life at that time for helping me to find opportunities in other challenges in my life.

I decided that I didn't want to be just a licenced Car Salesman, having to renew my licence every year; I wanted to become a Registered Car Salesman. This meant that I had a 12-part course to pass, normally taking twelve months to complete, but I did it in three. To get a quiet area in which to study, there were times when I did so in my car in the driveway. While I was doing this study, my practical education in all parts of the job also started.

I passed the exam gaining top marks in the region. As a result, it was decided that I should be elected to the Christchurch Branch of the Board of the Motor Vehicle Dealers Institute as a token female. Over the twelve months on the Board, I gained credibility and was re-elected to the Board the next year on my own merits. My job at the yard was now more car sales based. I found that I enjoyed the selling side of the job.

I left New Zealand to start a new life in Australia, moving to North Queensland. I applied for jobs as a car salesman only to be told that I had excellent references and if I was a man I would be employed on the spot- had I thought about cleaning cars!! In another, I was told that it was a choice between me and the town drunk-he got the job. I was up against gender bias in every role that I went for across the jobs I had experience in, and with all the determination in the world couldn't overcome that. It was the early eighties, and it was the town we had chosen to move to.

Fortunately, we moved to the Gold Coast after twelve months to start life afresh. Up North, I literally nearly lost my life due to a medical error; we lost everything we had financially after being conned in a business deal by supposed friends. It was a bit harder to find a positive out of all of this, but there were some.

After finding it difficult to get work up North, I had three large Car Sales firms all offer me employment. I agreed to start with one – I was about to go back into an environment that I enjoyed, but as it was new cars, not used, it would be very different from what I was experienced in. My start date was delayed as a new product was coming out and the boss wanted to train the staff. The delay changed the course of my life, as on the Friday before I was to start this job, I was also offered a job in a large corporation that I had applied for. I decided to take that one instead. It was my foot-in-the-door job, as I could see that it would lead to greater opportunities.

To keep me mentally active as well as working full time, I also took up full-time study at TAFE. My job was shift work, so this enabled me to juggle the two. When I look back, I am not sure how I did it but I certainly made the most of my opportunities. Over the next few years, I gained my Associate Diploma in Business Management and in Marketing. At the same time, taking opportunities job-wise, transferring between departments and gaining extra skills and knowledge across the organisation. In some areas, I was part of special teams; in others one of only two females in that business area. Eventually, I got back into an area that I enjoyed and was good at -sales. Selling to business customers over the phone. This then led to being out on the road selling to Business Customers face to face. Initially, I had a vast area going West to Ipswich and North to North Brisbane and, at times, the Sunshine Coast.

I only did this area for under a year as I saw that there would be an opportunity for me to work closer to home – short-term pain for long-term gain. From here, I travelled all over Australia in a training role within the same organisation. Allowing me to use my communication skills plus my coaching and mentoring skills. Then came the opportunity to work in a Regional Management role for twelve months while the role holder was on maternity leave. This was a stretch for me, and when I was given this opportunity, for whatever reason, I grabbed it with both hands, another chance to turn a challenge into an opportunity. I had a direct staff of 33 and an indirect of 150 – I thrived. I loved what I was doing, developing myself but, more importantly, getting the opportunity to develop others. Helping them to realise their potential.

At the same time, I was on the way up the corporate ladder. I was also developing as a leader in Toastmasters International, heading for the top Leadership opportunity within my District. Things were really looking up for me; my job, although time-consuming, was fulfilling, I was excelling as a manager, and my staff were thriving. I was in line for a national role. I had applied for a job in Sydney, which I had decided I would do during the week and return home to the Gold Coast at the weekend. Life was busy, but good everything was going my way. I didn't get the role which may well have saved my life as I followed through with a medical check and got something far more life-changing than any job would have been.

I was diagnosed with a rarer form of cancer, nothing ordinary for me, cancer of the nipple. I had surgery but didn't lose the breast, just the nipple, followed by 33 doses of radiation. Leadership within Toastmasters was not even on my radar anymore. I was still getting my head around planning a week in advance, let alone committing to plans that looked three to four years ahead.

Finding a positive in that challenge was a little harder, but I realised how lucky I was; I had been given the opportunity to realise what I had before it was gone. So many people aren't given that chance. I have found that people and situations come into my life at the right time. I was scheduled to do a Dale Carnegie course, and the books for it arrived before my diagnosis. One of them was How to Stop Worrying and Start Living. This book also helped me to get through the months ahead.

Life got back on to an even keel, and eighteen months after my first diagnosis, I was ready to go after some of my goals again. I set my sights on higher leadership within Toastmasters and was right into campaign mode again. Five months before election day, I was once again diagnosed with cancer, and this time my surgeon suggested that I have a mastectomy as a preventative measure. At the same time, my son was due to go on his overseas experience. I thought of delaying my operation so he wouldn't know of it. My surgeon suggested against this, though, so he left the day after my surgery. I think that was hard for both of us, but I didn't want him to forego his dreams.

I got to re-evaluate my life again and give thanks for the positives in it. I got to think about my own mortality and be reminded I wasn't immortal. I had the opportunity for redundancy from the Corporation because of my health, so I decided to take it and travel a new path- another opportunity from a challenge.

I followed another of my strengths and went into the Training arena, working for a Registered Training Organisation. I started in one role and then got the opportunity to move into another. In that role, I was fortunate enough to travel around Australia doing training, primarily training trainers to be trainers. I got to put all my skills to use in this role. As a trainer, I got the opportunity to help others to realise and unlock their potential. It could be demanding work, but it was very fulfilling, nurturing, and developing others. The most rewarding were those who doubted their potential for various reasons. Helping them to realise, develop and watch them grow and flourish.

At the same time, I became very involved with training within Toastmasters; another way I could use my skills to assist me further with this was I became a Myers Briggs Practitioner, becoming qualified in this area. Coupled with my understanding of learning styles, I added more tools to my toolbox. I decided to go into the Speech Contest side of the organisation and develop my own presentation skills even further. I became involved in leadership at a lower level and enjoyed being able to mentor and coach others.

Finally, after twenty years, I decided to go for one of my goals and stand for District leadership in Toastmasters. This time I wasn't held back by any unexpected health issues and was elected. In 2015 I became District Director of my District, which encompassed Queensland, Northern New South Wales, Northern Territory and Papua New Guinea. A whole lot of opportunities opened for me, giving me access to being trained at an international level and opening worldwide networks for me.

I am still actively involved in Toastmasters as I believe learning is lifelong. I can use the skills that I have gained, at a different level, as I support and mentor others. I have become actively involved in assisting in the development of Toastmasters in Papua New Guinea. I know that I can play a small part in developing the peoples of Papua New Guinea with their leadership and communication skills. I have been a regular visitor to Papua New Guinea to do this.

I have been fortunate enough to be associated with Papua New Guinea Australia Awards Alumni. An Alumni made up of Papua New Guineans who have gained Academic Qualifications and have been funded by Australian Awards to cover the cost of their expenses. Many have done their studies in Australia, but not all. They have all studied hard and, in many cases, overcome great hurdles to complete their studies. I feel very honoured to be able to assist them in growing their communication skills, finding their potential and the ability to be able to communicate more effectively in their chosen fields. They inspire me with their stories.

Working with the Alumni, I have travelled all over Papua New

Guinea. This is a country rich in culture and languages. There are over 840 different languages spoken within Papua New Guinea. Most Papua New Guineans can speak three languages, their tribal language, their form of pidgin and English. I am continually impressed with the people I work with as they realise the importance of the skills that I can assist them to gain. I have a great passion for what I am able to do there and consider it to be my legacy.

There has been a positive that has come from the recent pandemic, and that has been that we have all become more able to use different forms of communication since travel has been limited. Zoom and Teams have become a part of our lives, and it has enabled me to be able to have a further reach into areas of Papua New Guinea that I couldn't readily get into or support.

Recently I have become involved with the Gold Coast Innovation Hub. This initially started with my involvement in the starting of the GC Hub Toastmasters Club. I met the very dynamic CEO Sharon Hunneybell and Board member Steve Dalton. I used my skills to help with the development of the skills of the members of the Hub. I have assisted with some of the accelerators they have run, coaching the participants with the delivery of their pitches. I find these people very inspiring with all their ideas, and enjoying my coaching of them.

Gold Coast Female Founders are another group I have become involved with. Having Brunch with a room full of Female Founders is certainly a great way to lift any day. They are all striving to create opportunities out of the challenges faced. The gatherings are even more special for me when one of the speakers is someone I have coached, assisting them to tell their story.

What does the future look like for me? I have met several people along the way in my life's journey with who I am now looking to collaborate with as well as my current coaching; I will be expanding more in these areas of opportunity.

There is my beautiful friend Lisa who, along with her husband, has brought a property, a retreat, in Northern New South Wales. We will be combining our skills and running workshops at the property. I will be involved in Leadership, Sales and, of course, Speaking because if you can't tell it, you can't sell it. Communication really is the key to everything.

We will also run retreats as the place really is a Sanctuary and the ideal spot. These retreats will have limited places with some specialised designed for the corporate environment. I can't wait for Lisa and I to start this journey and assist others to find opportunities in their challenges, especially in the business world. Personal Development in Paradise what could be better.

As I believe in lifelong learning and practising it myself, I will also be strengthening my skills in that arena, having been presented with opportunities to collaborate with Registered Training Organisations.

Time to also step back into keynote speaking and increase my skills and exposure there so that I am also able to offer even more coaching to others wanting to also enter this field.

The opportunities for me are limitless as they are for anyone else. We all have challenges in our lives. It doesn't matter what they are in comparison to anyone else's challenges - for us; they can be huge. The most important thing is that there are always opportunities in challenges. Granted, sometimes they may be harder to find than others, but they are there.

I often think back to that ten-year-old child being encouraged to speak impromptu by her teacher, discovering that communication really has been my key to everything and also having the right people to coach and support me along the way.

This has helped to mould me into the person I am today, taking this opportunity to share some of my life's journey. with you. Looking forward to being able to enrich our connection even further as I assist you to find challenges in the opportunities in your lives. If you want coaching in Communication, Leadership or Sales, please contact me. Remember, if you can't tell it, you can't sell it, whatever that may be. I can tailor any coaching to you or your group.

Keep in mind those wise words from Winston Churchill 'Pessimists see challenges in every opportunity while optimists see opportunities in every challenge. Become an optimist like me – I am here to help you.

About the Author

Christine Lennon has been a trailblazer for women in business and sales for over 40 years. She is the first woman to become elected to the Board of the Motor Vehicle Dealer's Institute in New Zealand. She has since gone on to share her expertise in communication and sales with corporate and women leaders both here in Australia and internationally.

Christine is an active business coach and mentor, helping female founders through the Australian Female Founders program and running workshops and certification courses. She is also a proud leader of Toastmasters for over 25 years, empowering people through communication education. Christine's passion is to help others achieve their goals and create positive change in the world.

Email: chris@christinelennonconsulting.com
Website: christinelennonconsulting.com
LinkedIn: www.linkedin.com/in/christine-lennon-51a5863a/

Voices of Impact

Karen Macvicar

Dig your heels in

Motherwell to Clydebank was a train journey I'd never taken before. The huge inconvenience of my car breaking down forced me to take the 08:17 at Platform 3. This was a day where I was sure I would get my 10,000 steps as I had certainly not got anywhere near that in the last 2 weeks. Covid had caught up with my son just before the Christmas holidays in 2021, and we had to isolate together for 10 days. My teenage son, Ross, had no trouble at all, spending most of his days choosing between the Xbox, YouTube and computer games and very little school work. I'm sure there was more, but I was concerned about his cough and temperature. So managing not to catch Covid, I was delighted to be able to escape the 4 walls, where I'd spent lots of time thinking and sometimes overthinking.

During the 61-minute train journey, I had lots of time to look out the window on the sunny, frosty, cold morning and get lost in my thoughts. On 1st January, I'd written my goals; one was to read the Bible. I chose to use the Bible in One Year app, so headphones in, 23 minutes of listening to 'Battles and Blessings' where a husband had launched a successful ministry just as his wife was diagnosed with cancer.

Two days before my train journey, I signed a 6-month contract for a new job. I'd been given a book, 'If You Want to Walk on Water, You've Got to Get out of the Boat'; this new job was my attempt to tiptoe into the water before letting go of the boat. The previous summer, my local church had asked me to be the Mad Scientist at their holiday club to teach science experiments with a Bible-based theme. I loved the whole experience. Now this church had called me to be their children's ministry leader, and I also felt I was called to the position too and excited for the next 6 months of adventures.

Children's ministry had been part of my Sunday and occasionally mid-week service for years. I had been learning from the best, Nicola, Helen and Jim, who have lovingly devoted their time and God-given talents to so many children for a number of years.

I'd put my make-up on that morning, a new range I'd started exploring. Along with working as a chemist, on call as a scientific adviser, children's ministry and most importantly, a mum to a teenager. I had a 'side hustle' too but was struggling with it. One of my friends was selling a vegan skincare range, and the passion Gillian shared was endearing. One day early, October, I came to my Scottish 'ends tether'. I had got myself in debt again; it was almost my son's 14th birthday. I was supposed to be going on a trip that I couldn't afford and couldn't get my finances in order again. That morning I remember praying, what on earth shall I do, Lord? So I decided to say I couldn't go, no excuses, I just didn't have enough money. What a relief to admit it instead of putting it on my credit card.

This is a weirdly funny bit, Gillian had messaged me about an eye mask, and I hadn't replied, so weeks later, I remembered and replied that day I'd prayed. Gillian called me, and we got chatting about how I'd been getting on in my side hustle, honestly, not very well. What about trying Tropic, could I? It would be my 3rd network marketing company; what would people think? I liked the natural vegan products and the look of the products, but what would people say? I agreed to have a look at it, and as I drove home from work, I burst into tears, having a wee self-pity party. That morning, I asked God to show me a way out of my money worries; I felt God saying, there you are, I've got you starting the conversation; now decide what you're doing now. My tears dried up at the thought of an answered prayer. The next day in my car, I found a Tropic brochure down the side of my driving seat from Gillian; the answer had been under my nose for weeks. So that started my self-care journey of cleansing my face, experimenting with makeup, using body washes, scrubs, and lotions, and even being adventurous with fake tan; being Scottish, my natural shade is pale blue. My 51-year young body was enjoying all the attention it had missed for years.

As I got nearer Clydebank, I started to think about what had brought me to this appointment. I kept losing my voice and had awful indigestion. The acid caused damage to my vocal cords, and I was told not to speak for 2 weeks. This was a huge learning for me, people would shout at me, and treat me as if I couldn't hear, understand, and speak slowly, and I was sometimes left out of conversations as I couldn't contribute. I know this was not on purpose; I think people didn't know how to react. I was also advised that I shouldn't sing, shout or whisper for 6 months. Things were beginning to be a bit emotionally challenged for me, and I was feeling as if I was being gently separated from things I loved doing. Have you ever had to stay silent when you wanted to sing or scream at the top of your voice? This taught me to evaluate my reactions to situations.

So off I went to my hospital appointment, an abdomen ultrasound, and then back to my work in the laboratory in Glasgow. My car was in the garage, so I collected it, all fixed, from Motherwell after work that day, 14,231 steps later. I'd just got in the car and started the engine, and my phone rang. It was my doctor's phone number; that's unusual, I thought. 'Karen, the ultrasound of your abdomen today has revealed a 5 cm suspicious tumour in your left kidney'. I felt my insides implode at that moment, sitting in my freezing cold car, in the darkness of a winter's night, my whole body shaking, kidney, tumour, really? I have Lupus, and my kidney function was tested last month, and it was ok. This made no sense at all.

What about my son, my family, my friends, my new job, my, my, my, my selfish thoughts had got me into a spiral of such fear of the unknown. That night I kept falling asleep and waking up with the words of the doctor in my ears. I also had a song in my heart, 'The Joy of the Lord is my Strength' by Rend Collective, and as I looked out of my bedroom, I kept my eyes on the framed picture of a lighthouse with the words of The Footprints poem. Reminding me in situations, there is one set of Footprints, and you are the one being carried.

For 26 years, I've been a scientific adviser, being on call to attend emergency chemical incidents. I now felt like I was attending my own emergency incident.

I had just entered the phase when my pager going off, and getting the first piece of information. Knowing that this isn't always the full picture, you still try to put the pieces together and make decisions about what to do next.

This emergency phase involved lots of phone calls to family and close friends, putting my new job on hold, and not working in the laboratory either. I felt stuck in disbelief. Being on call, an incident can happen anytime; I was 'on call' for this incident since I'd lost my voice and waiting to find out what was causing it.

It was the timing of it all that got me; I thought I was supposed to start tip-toeing in the water of a new ministry. I was convinced I was doing the right thing; why was this happening now? What about my new skincare venture and who was going to do my work in the laboratory? Living with Lupus, I'd been used to being aware my wee body could turn on me at any point, but I'm good to my body, so why did it decide to behave badly? Had I personally done something to my kidney, exposed myself to chemicals, or done something I shouldn't have, the questions in my head were weird and consuming. Strangely, I did not google anything; I didn't want to know more than I needed to at this stage.

The next phase arriving at the incident, knowing it's a real job and needs further assessment. My doctor told me I was on the urgent care list; the renal consultant would be in touch to arrange to follow-up tests. This was like waiting around for a key holder of a premise to arrive to gain access. The door didn't need to be forced open, but we couldn't leave the incident until the full area had been checked out.

In this time of waiting, we had lots of family time, walks, and people praying. Honestly, I found it difficult to pray, it was like an internal ache, but I was assured other people were praying for me. But I didn't lose hope and knew God was holding my hand.

An initial phone call from the consultant indicated that it looked like a cancer tumour and could have been in my body for years. I would need a CT scan to see if it had spread before further decisions were made. We prayed for a quick scan and got one on a Sunday, my favourite day, my friends said. When I sat up after the scan, I remember the nurse placing her hand on my left shoulder and just pausing and looking at me. Do nurses pray for you? Did she see something in my scan that she knew wasn't right?

One morning I was making soup for my son; I couldn't go to work, I just wanted to be at home for my son. I decided to listen to videos I'd received in an email from Fire Fighters for Christ. Mark Hall, from Casting Crowns, was talking about having terrible indigestion and a sore back; he got a CT scan and found out he had renal cancer. In his disbelief and overwhelming emotions, he wrote the song, Oh My Soul, after his diagnosis. I looked at my cooker and noticed a note I had written on a magnet on 5th January 2020 with the title of that song; I'd sand it so many times before. I had been told on 5th January 2022, after my ultrasound, that I potentially had renal cancer, 2 years after I'd written the note.

I also went for healing ministry and prayer walks and tried lots of Tropic products to help pamper myself and encourage other women to take more care of themselves. Distracting myself by making more skincare and makeup videos. Looking back at my videos before diagnosis was weird as it didn't look like anything was going on in my body, I still didn't understand, and do we ever really take it all in? Doing short videos was something I had to learn. Don't take yourself too seriously; you were not supposed to be perfect. People want to see the real you. 'I love your wee videos with your calming voice' is often a comment I gratefully receive.

Learning to do these came from advice initially from Melanie Wood from Speaking Styles when she did a free seminar in Glasgow to have confidence in public speaking. Then with Brynn Lang, where I invested to learn techniques for network marketing and 'press the darn button' when going live on Facebook. Watching The Cheerleader of Dreams, Terri Savelle Foy, on Facebook, helped me to learn to say over and over, 'I am fit, firm, and in the best shape of my life and cancer free'. And to pray big prayers when I had no idea what the outcome would be.

Will all the information was collected, and the plan of action was to remove my kidney; the tumour looked contained. On my operation day, 7th March, I walked in with my bright pink jogging suit, ready to face whatever the next few hours or days would be. I met the consultant, signed the papers and took the medication and just like that, I had to trust it would be ok. 4 hours later, I woke up, minus the offending organ, the keyhole surgery had removed the blocked waterworks, and I felt as if I'd had done 3000 sit-ups. I remember the next day and I met my nurses that would look after me. A few attempts to get me up were not pleasant, and I was left to rest until the next day. I woke up, and I had slid down to the bottom of the bed. My nurse told me in a firm but gentle voice, dig your heels in. I just wanted to curl up and wake up when I was feeling alive and at home with my son. So, I had a choice, look down and stay down or look up and push myself up the bed. A few centimetres at a time, I pushed myself, I got up and out of the bed, and one step at a time, I managed to walk up the corridor of the ward; it did take me 4 days to have the strength to do this. And to this day, when I feel a bit lost, overwhelmed, and wondering what it's all about, I can hear my nurse saying, dig your heels in, Karen, and look up.

In the clean-up phase, when the handover occurs, it's no longer an emergency. Kylie, my good kidney, or should I call her 'I should be so Lucky' kidney, although missing her twin, was performing her duties well. On day 4, I was allowed to go home; my wee brother wheeled me out of the hospital and took me home. My mum stayed with me for a while and welcomed all the visitors from family and friends with cups of tea, biscuits and of course cakes. My dad always had a joke to tell me and keep me smiling through each day. Your family and friends, and work colleagues go through more than you imagine; grateful and thankful seem such small words in comparison to their generosity in time and kindness.

Then the de-brief, oh, there were many of them, and they can be mentally challenging telling your story. And getting the results from my cancer nurse to the conclusion of the pathology of the tumour. Low-grade cancer, yearly ultrasound for Kylie and chest x-ray for my lungs. Should I give my lungs a name? Getting help from Maggies Cancer Centre and Look Good Feeling Better charities was incredible. One day I sat with a group of brave ladies at different stages of our cancer journey and learned to put on makeup with confidence. Also, styling with confidence, and ladies were talking about wigs to wear and scarfs to hide their mastectomy, and I randomly said I couldn't get my jeans on because of my swollen tummy and the waistband sitting on my biggest scar. We all laughed; it's good to laugh; no, it's wonderful to be able to laugh with other ladies who are on their own journey. In any incident, there is trauma to recover from, and laughter is the best medicine and positive mindset.

So that's me back on call again for chemical incidents and in the back of my mind for another 'body chemical incident'. And 9 months on from diagnosis, the children's ministry has started. In those 9 months of twists and turns, there had been a change in me physically, mentally and spiritually for the better.

There have been meetings and speaking with people I would

never have had conversations with. Losing my voice and the difficulty in communication, and the way people treat you when you can't speak, has encouraged me to learn British Sign Language. Maybe there will be children or parents in my future ministry or my skincare business that are deaf; who knows? You still have a voice if you are deaf. Being involved in the Voices of Impact is more poignant now, as losing my voice and discovering the tumour that had been growing for years. There is much more detail of this story I'd like to share in podcasts or speaking engagements to encourage women to accept and love themselves with physical and mental scars.

I'd love to continue with my skincare business and be able to expand it with a team of like-minded people. Develop makeup techniques for older women to give them the confidence to know how beautiful they are. Every day is a beauty school day, and creating videos are fun, learning to love yourself, top to toe. Tropic skincare kept me going physically to take care of my body and cherish my scars, which sometimes cause my eyes to well up when I catch a glimpse of them in the mirror. Spiritually my faith has been stretched and moulded in a way I'd never expected; Proverbs 3 verse 5-6, Trust in the Lord with all your heart, has a whole new meaning now. And continue using science to share my faith; to me, God is the best scientist.

I've started listening to Bible App again, and I'd just been through my Battles and Blessings, was that story on the train a sign of what I was about to go through?

Battles and Blessings can run together; learn to be thankful for not only your blessings but the battles you face; they make you the person you will grow to love more and more. So put on your armour, as you are fearfully and wonderfully made.

About the Author

Karen Macvicar is a single mum to a teenager, a scientist, children's ministry leader, and she loves learning new ways of caring for herself and others, physically, mentally and spiritually.

Born and bred in Bonnie, Scotland, and grew up near Glasgow. Her first words in the morning as she lifts the covers off are 'Good Morning Lord, what adventures are we going to have today'. She always takes the front seat in the rollercoaster of life where the ups and downs and twisted turns have made her check that the seat belt has been tightly fastened. When she gets to the end of the journey, her hands will be lifted high in the victory of surviving the rollercoaster of her life.

Karen rekindled her passion for drawing and painting and loves an Empire Biscuit as a treat and walking in the local woodlands' estate with her son when they have their 'blethering time'.

Email: Karenmacvicar@gmail.com
Facebook: Karen Macvicar
Website: www.tropicskincare.com/pages/karenmacvicar

Cattalia Lee Montgomery

Confessions of an Ex-Doormat Empath

I confess I was a drama addict and a full-blown course junkie. I confess I was an eternal student, seeking yet another technique to give me the confidence I needed to be the healer I was called to be.

I confess that my life was a bloody mess at age 42, with 3 failed marriages, 1 finished and 3 half-finished university degrees and one million, one hundred healing qualifications under my belt. I couldn't figure out how to change it.

I eventually realised I was stuck in a doormat empath self-sabotage cycle, continuously distracted and thrown off course from my goals by the destructive relationships and situations I got into. This is the story of how I escaped this harmful cycle.

Let me take you back to where it all started at sweet 16 with my first true love. A possessive, controlling, unhinged young man who cheated on me with his ex-girlfriend. Honestly, I believed his behaviour was just something I had to put up with because 'I loved him'. I tried to break up with him when I awoke from this spell. In true psychopath style, he threatened to kill me, so I had to take a restraining order out on him. He said I would never get away from him, but luckily I did. For a while at least, as I would relive this same relationship with different men, over and over, on and off, for the next 25 years.

Enter stage right, my first husband. An out-of-work, wanna-be actor and pathological liar who couldn't hold down a job. After only 3 months, he cheated on me with my maid of (dis)honour, and I was utterly humiliated.

A few years later came husband number 2, the evangelical born-again Christian. This was by far the worst relationship I have ever been in. He watched and controlled my every move and ridiculously accused me of having affairs (even when I was pregnant). His constant attacks on my self-esteem drove me close to suicide. I tried to get away several times, but he used the 'widow with the young child' card to guilt me into returning. I felt so responsible for his grieving 3-year-old son that I would always return. I guess I needed to be needed more than I needed to be loved.

I received a wake-up call when my own son was born. I knew deep within that I couldn't be a good mother to him if I stayed with his Dad. I was grappling with postnatal depression and experiencing the polar opposite of love and support. So, I left with my 6-week-old babe in my arms to try to get well. The harassment and revenge leveled at me for the next 6 years were intense and hard to navigate.

However, I was determined to be a good mother and wanted to ensure I never got into another relationship like this in the future. Not just for my sake but my son's.

So, I began a quest, a journey of spiritual exploration and self-discovery. I dove deep into my psyche. I uncovered my early childhood wounds and the sexual abuse. I slowly realised the dysfunction in my family and upbringing, which had brought me to a place of very low self-esteem and never feeling good enough, resulting in zero boundaries and over-involving myself in others' dramas. I realised I felt compelled to save EVERYONE when really I needed to save ME.

A Kinesiologist introduced me to the word Narcissistic. "Not all bruises are on the outside," he said about my situation, and suddenly the madness that was my marriage made sense. I had experienced narcissistic abuse. I was not a crazy woman with anger issues, as he made me believe.

For the first time, I felt real hope for my future. Implementing the strategies of Grey Rock and No to Low Contact helped me hold on to my sanity as he continued to use co-parenting, child support and divorce settlement as tools of access, conflict and control.

Six fun-filled years later, I decided I was ready for another relationship. I wanted to see how far I had come. I was pretty confident that I loved myself now, and I knew what my woundings were. I had healed myself of a pain condition called vulvodynia (a result of sexual abuse), and I believed I was ready!

Enter stage left, husband number 3. On our first date, he told me he used to be a gambling addict and had done some crazy things to support his addiction. I should have run, but he claimed to have done the recovery work, and it was no longer a problem for him. I was impressed, and I thought that since I had done my recovery work, too, I was safe. Sadly, I was mistaken. He was testing me and 100% lying.

Regrettably, I fell pregnant with him 2 months in. I shuddered at the thought of being a single mum AGAIN. So, I did what any scared woman would do to survive... I shut down my awareness and ignored the many red flags before me. I had to make this relationship work.

After a few years with him, I became depressed and drank A LOT. I couldn't understand his dark moods and why he picked fights so much. He was adept at projecting his pain and shame onto me. He even accused me of being responsible for our bad financial situation.

One day he was violent towards my eldest son, and I decided to leave. I opened my inner eyes and soon discovered his betrayals. Not only had he NEVER stopped gambling, but he had cheated on me with his ex-girlfriend when I was 8 months pregnant. I finally admitted that he was not a good husband.

I kicked him out and dove deeper into healing from Narcissistic Abuse, determined to end this doormat empath self-sabotage cycle once and for all. This time I was stronger and prepared for the hostilities that ensued. He didn't seem to be as bad as my second husband.

The next important concept I learned on my healing journey was that the Empath and the Narcissist are two extremes existing at opposite ends of the SAME self-love spectrum. Both are extremely dysfunctional, afraid and controlled in their own way. Each is attracted to the equal but opposite end of the spectrum. I now knew there were multiple types of Narcs of varying degrees. Hence, husband number 3 wasn't as obvious or bad as number 2.

The extreme Doormat Empath has little to no boundaries, self-esteem or self-love. They don't know how to love or be loved, only to be needy and needed.

The extreme Narc is also incapable of love, is emotionally empty and incredibly self-centred. They are incapable of holding feelings of shame or guilt. To them, it feels like death, and they avoid it at all costs. They are experts at projecting these emotions instead onto the nearest empath.

Most people fall somewhere along the two sides of this Self-Love Spectrum.

Both disordered personalities are created by experiencing varying degrees of alcoholic, dissociated, and/or narcissistic parents. Interestingly, each holds the other's medicine.

The Empath needs to learn to be more selfish, to love themselves, do less for others and take care of themselves. The Narc needs to learn empathy, compassion for others, and REAL love for themselves.

Narcs, unfortunately, are largely unable and unwilling to change as they believe there is NOTHING wrong with them. On the other hand, an empath has more of a chance to change as they believe EVERYTHING is wrong with them.

As we heal, we shift towards the middle of the spectrum. In the centre is the person with healthy levels of self-love and self-worth; they give and receive freely and flexibly in relationships, having healthy boundaries. This person does not attract or suffer doormat empaths or narcissists as partners or friends. They are simply not a vibrational match for them.

As an empath moves towards the middle of the continuum, they attract a partner from the narc side who is closer to the centre. My mission was to move as close to the centre as possible.

To help you also on your way towards the centre of that self-love spectrum, I am gifting to you a FREE 5D energy tool. To transmute negative feelings and emotions that you may have towards yourself, others and situations www.tinyurl.com/2p8hyf48

Aside from my broken marriages, I had a pattern of half-finishing degrees and took course after course as I mentioned earlier.

As the first person in our family to go to university, my mother ensured I followed her unlived dream of working in public relations and media. My dream, however, was to be a nurse.

My heart was not in my public relations degree, and my increasingly bad grades made me believe I would never make it in the real world. It reinforced my belief that there was something wrong with me.

After my 2nd divorce, during my healing journey, I learned and practised many different modalities... Reiki Master, Isis Seichim Master, Psychic Surgery, Astro-Chakra Synergy System, Holographic Kinetics, Shamanic Midwifery, Doula, Midwifery, Hypnobirthing, Pregnancy Yoga, Birth into Being (rebirthing), Neurolinguistic Kinesiology, Hypnosis, EFT, Voice Dialogue, & Organ Regeneration.

And as I said before, I started 3 different university degrees - Career Counselling (ironic, I know), Midwifery and Chiropractic. I stopped exactly halfway through each for various dramatic reasons.

After my 3rd shame-inducing divorce, I decided I needed to get my act together as a healer. I had two young boys to support on my own now. I could never see myself getting married again, so I had to earn good money on my own to survive. I wanted to be respected and make it in the world. This was when I began my journey toward Chiropractic. While studying Chiropractic, I also learnt 3 related modalities – Neural Organisation Technique, Bio-Geometric Integration, & Spinal Flow.

Despite my plethora of skills, knowledge and experience, I still felt extremely unsure of myself. I kept looking for that next modality to give me the final piece I needed. That skill would make me finally believe I was ready to make it as a healer full-time. So far, I hadn't made it much past working on family and friends. I just didn't have the confidence, and I was OVER IT.

Then one day, I found the key, Creatrix® Transformology®. It guaranteed to get rid of the blocks that were holding me back and get LASTING results. I didn't have the money or time to do it at first, and I wasn't sure it would work for me. So far, NOTHING had. But I just knew that Creatrix® was different, and I was determined to make it happen. I was determined to turn my life around. And I did.

Creatrix® changed EVERYTHING. My confidence in myself and my healing abilities became radically different. The voice in my head telling me I didn't know what I was doing was silent; the fear that I was a fraud was gone. Bye-bye, Imposter Syndrome. New thoughts would effortlessly fill my head, like "of course, you can do this", "you get amazing results", "you know what you are doing", and "whatever healing you give is EXACTLY what your client needs at this moment." I felt so calm and confident. Even my sweaty palms disappeared.

For the first time EVER, I began working in a proper clinic, not my spare bedroom, as a Spinal Flow Practitioner. I had regular full-paying clients. I joined a business networking group and spoke about what I did as a proper businesswoman. To my amazement, I saw that everyone else was just like me. There was no significant difference between these successful business people and me.

My life became so much more peaceful. For instance, I became a very calm mother and didn't get excessively triggered by my ex's anymore. My extreme studying stress and exam nerves TOTALLY disappeared to the point where I worried that I would fail. But instead, my grades actually improved. Best of all, I gained the courage to start an amazing new relationship.

I am now in a loving marriage which nurtures and uplifts my soul. We adore, respect, and care for each other equally. I no longer accept narcissistic abuse in my life (including friends and family).

I am no longer a doormat empath; I am now a CONFIDENT and POWERFUL Healer.

I was so blown away by my transformation that I became a Creatrix® Transformologist® myself to help other women be FREE like me. Free from the doormat empath self-sabotage cycle.

My life purpose now is to Creatrix® and Coach Healers. I am a Healer of Healers if you like.

One of my first clients was Paige, an experienced and highly intuitive Kinesiologist practitioner and teacher. She had relationship issues, feeling unsupported by her partner and getting frustrated daily with their 3 rambunctious young boys. But mostly, she felt like something was holding her back in her business. She wasn't getting enough clients or making the money that she wanted.

After Creatrix, she stopped comparing herself to others, got rid of feeling not good enough, resolved issues around rejection and much, much more. Immediately she could ask for and receive the support she needed without the emotional drama it used to entail.

She was calmer with her children and no longer negatively compared herself with other mothers or practitioners. Most amazingly, she was able to start a new healing business during the pandemic, which made more money than she had ever made in any of her other businesses. To this day, she is growing and achieving more and more. Nothing is holding her back.

Another client is the talented naturopath/healer, M. She was stuck in the middle of trying to write her book. "How to Sizzle in your 70s." She was full of excuses, distractions and inaction. She was the quintessential doormat empath, burdened with looking after a house full of grown men who took her for granted. She waited hand-and-foot on them all. Her man-child husband, her cranky older brother, and her mentally and emotionally challenged 40-something son.

M was tired and depressed but really wanted more. After her Creatrix sessions, I hadn't heard from her in months. I had moved interstate, and we lost touch. I was worried until she resurfaced, saying, "sorry I haven't been in contact; I locked myself away and finished my book. I'm getting divorced, and I am selling my house." Last I saw, she was posting on FB about having a marvellous time at an international writers' conference in Sydney. Wow!

Another favourite success story is Michelle. A talented, intuitive healer and creative. She had a long history of trauma - her first husband died young, and she suffered from extreme anxiety and low self-esteem. Michelle worked in a crystal & healing centre. The owners agreed to sell her unique handmade necklaces and also offered their healing rooms to practice from. However, she kept finding excuses not to finish her creations, and she was too nervous to promote her healing offerings. To top it all off, this talented musician with a gorgeous voice was too shy to sing in her own shower in case the neighbours heard her.

Michelle went through my signature program, where I guide women healers to the confidence level of a master practitioner. We "Creatrixed" her anxiety, the belief she was not good enough and much, much more. I also inducted her into the powerful 5D Kinesiology modality of Bodyflow Energetics, which enhanced the skills and gifts that she already possessed.

Michelle no longer lives in a state of constant anxiety. Which she hadn't realised was so bad until it was gone. Her new challenge is re-stocking her creations in the shop, as they constantly sell out. She has to limit the private bespoke orders to keep up. She confidently promotes her healing abilities and provides her powerful and unique healing sessions in the practitioner rooms at the centre. The voice in her head now says, "of course, I can." And she sings her heart out in the shower and doesn't care if anyone hears her.

These are just 3 inspiring examples of the many transformation stories of women overcoming their negative relationship issues and blasting through confidence barriers to success by releasing trauma and changing their negative beliefs. It is such a joy to be doing this work, and I give thanks every day that this is now my life's work.

My wonderful husband (a Chiropractor & spiritual healer) and I recently launched the Inspired Freedom Academy in response to the pandemic. We ourselves needed to pivot to work online, retain our freedom and continue to serve others in a healing capacity. We feel called to empower others to do this as well. So not only do we help healers of all sorts break through to success, but we show them how to do it from anywhere in the world online.

Our goal is to create a tribe of powerful, confident Healers who support each other to stand in their truth, heal generations of trauma and assist in Humanity's Ascension.

Unlike other modalities, we do not only give you another technique/skill set. We take you on a full transformation journey, developing ALL the skills you need for SUCCESS inside and out. And so, I invite you inside the Inspired Freedom Academy if you are called to be an Impactful & Abundant Healer. Book a connection call with me www.cattalia.youcanbook.me. You can break the cycle too, have an unshakeable confidence and stop wasting money on endless courses!

About the Author

Cattalia is the co-founder and owner of the Inspired Freedom Academy and the better half of Dr Marshal & Cattalia @ drmcatt.com. Over the years, she has helped many women to become confident, impactful and abundant healers.

She lives in outback Qld with her husband Marshal and youngest son Byron. Together they enjoy caretaking the 5000-acre farm they live on, with many horses, cows, wallabies, chickens and guinea fowl.

When she is not healing, coaching and inspiring women to level up, she loves to explore the outdoors, excels in archery, grows food and enjoys the gorgeous burnt orange sunsets every night. Her dream is to create a massive tribe of powerful, confident healers ready to play big and shift the world out of the 3D/4D drama control system into the higher dimensional realities of love and freedom that are available to us now.

Facebook: www.facebook.com/cattalia.lee
Website: www.drmcatt.com
Website: www.inspiredfreedom.academy

Voices of Impact

Jodi Porteous

When I was a kid, family was everything. All of our holidays were together, we spent a lot of time with extended family, and we would be described as close-knit. At the time, it was awesome, but looking back, I can see it was because we never had a lot of money – as a single-income family, we grew a lot of our own food and lived off the land (food grown on the farm) and made do with a lot of things. There were a lot of things we couldn't do, but there was also a lot we did do, and nothing that was important was missed. On holidays we played board games and played cards, did puzzles and problem solving and hanging out with each other. Holidays look a lot different now, with various different locations, accommodations and excursions, but when it comes down to it, our close-knit family unit is the most important thing to me.

I chose accounting as my career choice because my maths teacher in year 9 said it was a challenge. Once Uni finished, I applied for my first job, and when I heard the words out of my mouth, "I would like to be a partner one day", in my first interview at an accounting firm, it shocked me as I had never thought about it before. I got the job and worked towards becoming the best accountant that I could be. After working for 2 years in Perth, my then-boyfriend got a job offer in Karratha.

I had no idea where Karratha was; all I knew was that it was up north in Western Australia. It helped that both Aaron and myself were from small country towns, so we were not scared of moving to a remote area. In early 2002 we packed up everything we had and relocated with our 2 cats to Karratha, committed to two years with his employer in Karratha. By the time that two years were up, I had an opportunity to buy into Northwest Accountancy, and at the age of 24, I owned a part of an accounting business. I had been an accountant for 3.5 years. My spontaneous declaration at my first job interview at the end of 1999 resulted in achieving that goal because of the opportunities of being in the right place at the right time.

I learned a lot about running a business, meeting clients and providing tax & business advice, as well as preparing tax returns, keeping up with all of the required Continuing Professional Development and working with my fellow business owners. I only had a few weeks off work each time I gave birth to my 2 boys in 2005 and 2008, and they often worked with me in the office, sitting at spare desks and eating all of the biscuits in the kitchen.

In 2015, one of the teachers at the local high school asked me to present a class to the year 9 students about money management and taxes. I jumped at the chance to share my knowledge. I created some resources and activities to help open up the discussion about money. (I still use one of these activities now). I was also approached by the Library to teach a "budgeting 101" session, which I then turned into a "budgeting for families" workshop. Being in the room listening to kids chatting with their parents about what they wanted to do and buy when they were older was fascinating, and then contributing to the discussion made my heart sing. But then I'd go back to doing tax returns and my normal business as usual.

Meeting with all types of people throughout the years, I could see a lot of the money issues, from the plentiful times of the booms to the hard times of redundancies, market crashes and businesses struggling to keep their doors open. Businesses went broke and had to shut down as the last straw of not being able to pay staff after they had already racked up debts to the ATO and sometimes were behind on rent and other payments too. Every time one of my clients had their heart broken by a decision that affected their finances, I could see that it affected their mental health, not only for that person but their family, extended families and colleagues at work. I have seen marriage breakdowns, suicides, and people having to sell all their assets and start again and leave town with nothing. My clients felt stuck, and I didn't know how to help them. The ripple effect throughout the community was huge.

When July hit each year, I would work lots of hours and prepare hundreds of tax returns while trying to take advantage of the great weather and go camping or fishing on the rare weekend off. However, by 2017 / 2018, I started to think about what else is available to me. How can we support our business clients when all I am doing is tax returns? "Tax season" sucked up so much of our lives – late nights, Saturdays, and I was too tired to do anything else. I remember going to work and crying most days during tax season. I was a full-time working mum working 32-35 hours a week and doing most of the household jobs. I felt stuck. My mental health suffered, and I was a volatile boss and parent, at times yelling at my staff & my kids. Whenever I was in a bad mood, the atmosphere permeated the entire office, and everyone had to tiptoe around for fear that I would snap. Although I could see it, I didn't know how to fix it. I didn't know how to say no to tax returns, especially when I was constantly booked for 3 weeks in advance, from 2nd July all the way through to the end of October. It sucked the life out of me. So I started looking for other options… how could I support my clients and help them out?

I wanted to start to be more proactive rather than reactive to support my clients, and then Life Coaching found me. I signed up to take coaching lessons as well as learn a 12-month program that I could teach to others, focusing on goal setting and taking action, as well as working on my own personal development. This was brand new to me. I had only ever heard about Professional Development, where you learn more to help your career. Now I was exposed to Personal Development, so there was much personal growth for me. Around the same time, I took a trip to Fiji for a Business Chicks conference. I had never been overseas by myself before nor spent this much money on something that was not 100% work-related. As I was going all that way, I decided to add a few nights to the end of the trip to stay in a tiny island hotel by myself. This allowed me some space to unwind and relax all on my own. During this time, I drafted a 6-week course that would help families learn more about how to manage their money. As a mum and the money manager in the house, I felt the burden of managing the money, and at times it was hard. I wanted to share the newly acquired skills I had in coaching and teaching people money management so that it would help those holding the burden for their families as well, getting the whole family involved and having conversations about their current situation as well as being able to plan for the future.

After I read Barefoot Investor (by Scott Pape), the penny dropped. Two things hit home the most – ditch the credit card and stop paying interest when you can afford to pay the loan off. Finally, we had a purpose for our money. At times I was stressed about our household funds because we would spend too much on holidays or on another fun toy and still had bills to pay. We decided that paying down our debts will be a priority, so that work was no longer a "must do" but rather a "want to" suddenly we knew what we were doing with our excess funds. We worked out that if we could put extra money aside for the loans, we would be debt free within 10 years. This didn't stop us from having fun, though. We still had boats, kayaks, camper trailers, four-wheel drives and the best backyard in the Pilbara to use it all in. We didn't implement all of the accounts of the Barefoot Investor, because I already taught people how to manage their money and thought we were doing ok.

As I reduced the number of hours I prepared tax returns, I stepped up to do more of what I loved – training and teaching – and then I heard about Profit First. This was the solution to cash management that I didn't know existed. It's a bit like Barefoot Investor but for businesses, making sure that businesses always have enough money put aside for bills, wages, staff, taxes, profit and most importantly themselves. I signed up to be a Profit First Professional, and this springboarded my learning of my skills in helping my clients. This significantly improved my business, and I changed how I worked; I hired a business manager to help manage clients rather than try to do it all myself.

Around Christmas 2019, one of my husband's colleagues committed suicide. After he passed, it was Aaron's job to review all of his emails, and it seemed that there was financial pressure and unpaid bills that may have been one of the stresses that lead to his death. He earned good money, and if someone earning this sort of money can still have financial pressures and live from pay to pay and get so stressed there seems to be no way out, then I have a duty to educate people, to help them make better choices and to set up their finances so that they can move forward and not stay stuck. I declared that it would be his legacy to promote my services and help people who earned good money to stop wasting their money and be more on top of their finances. Mental health is a huge issue in remote areas – and I think some of it comes from not feeling like there is control over aspects of life such as how money is used and what you do at work, and how it impacts the way you live your life.

A couple of years ago, we implemented a system where each person in our household (including the kids) had their own bank account with a card and a set amount for the things they needed, like clothes, shoes, fun, plus a bit of extra spending money. My husband, who used to frustrate me with his spontaneous purchases that sometimes impacted how much was left for bills, now has his own money with a budget allocated. The mindset of having my own money has changed my understanding of money management. It is money for me to choose what I want to do, grab an ice cream, buy flowers, buy new clothes or shoes… and I can spend it or save it and be guilt-free. It is joy and fun and no risk because it's not going to impact the household budget and risk how much money is available for bills and debt repayments. This has been one of the biggest impacts on my family and me, as well as with other families I teach, to provide freedom and less stress for them, even if it's $20 each per week.

As I help clients to implement Profit First in their businesses, I find that there is a simple structure that they use to easily talk about bringing money into the business, reducing expenses, and spending money in the right areas. One of the foundations of Profit First is that the business always makes a profit, which is like a family budget having a buffer or emergency fund. When businesses aren't cash-strapped, owners start to invest more in their business and themselves, paying themselves a decent wage, and start saving for the future, and, best of all, starting to have a life outside of the business. I find the same with families. By making sure that the family has a buffer account in case of emergencies, as well as a chance to spend on themselves in a way that suits them, it gives freedom to think about more than just working to make ends meet… but rather having a way to enjoy themselves.

In our family, this is what we are doing now. There's a focus on reducing debt so that our next stage of life will be semi-retirement – to do work that we want to do so that we don't have to make big bucks to make the mortgage payments but rather top up income to give us something to do that we love while having fun. We are investing in different things (assets, personal & professional development) so that we can make more money for the future but also enjoy what we are doing now - I love finding adventures for myself at the weekends. Having a structure for our money so that we can make quick decisions about what's important and where we want to make changes to allocations, it keeps things simple. The great thing about the structure we use is that it's easy and quick to check and tweak every few months, and we can take advantage of opportunities that pop up and realign priorities when life throws curveballs at us.

As interest rates continue to change, we are keeping in front of our home loan payments by paying more than the minimum amount as well as using offset accounts to keep funds available for new opportunities. We use a financial adviser to help with shares, managed fund investments and super, and we chat regularly about what we want for the future and make plans to ensure that as many of our dreams we have can come true, which makes keeping to our allocated funds for bills and essentials really easy because we want to achieve our goals.

As I continue living my life, I have learned these lessons:

- when you are feeling uncomfortable with something, listen to it to find out what's going on to see what needs to change
- when you feel stuck, it's time to start thinking about the possibilities rather than dwelling on the negative current situation

- even if you think you are doing OK, there are probably some small tweaks you can make that will make a huge difference
- when you have a focus and something to aim for, there's something in the future to look forward to, you can stop dwelling on the uncomfortable now and start taking action
- the action creates confidence. So many people aren't confident with managing their money and so are stuck in the feast and famine cycle of getting paid and then spending it all straight away… and don't know how to structure their finances so that some can be put aside for an emergency, or be used for investing in your future
- do something that you love each day, week and month, and build it into part of your budget so that you are living, investing and celebrating all of the time
- budgeting can be expansive (i.e. providing growth and abundance), not just restrictive

To transform from being an accountant to being a Money Management Coach, I set up a business called Intentional Money Management Pty Ltd, with the philosophy that if everyone was more intentional with their money, there would be less stress and more rewards. I teach the practical skills of money management and guide my clients through a series of activities to help them get their families on the same page and think about the future together, to be connected and driven by the same goals to keep each other accountable.

The business is all online, meaning that I can help more clients across Australia and the world by being able to watch and learn together as a couple, where there's common ground to have meaningful conversations, be inspired and take action towards living together in harmony. I want other families to have what we have – the ability to quickly manage the household budget, to easily tweak it when things crop up and make the most of every day. But mostly, I want people to understand that life's not just about work and making money to pay the bills. Life's about living. Being happy with what you have now, while working towards creating a life that you both love living together.

My mission is to impact 200 families a year by providing the skills and resources to get couples on the same page. To help reduce mental health issues by giving couples the connection to each other, by understanding what's important to each person in the relationship and by giving them tools to set up the purpose for their funds to live a meaningful life together.

If you are struggling to connect with your partner regarding finances, then I'd love for you to join my free webinar and Make Your Money Matter. My hope for you is that you can enhance your relationships with your partner and your money so that you can create your life just how you want it.

About the Author

Jodi Porteous is a Money Management Coach who works with couples to set up their finances that work in a way that works for them so that they can set up for their future together without compromising their current lifestyle. She is an accountant and tax agent with over 20 years of experience and a Certified Profit First Professional specialising in bringing the concept of household budgeting.

Jodi has lived in Western Australia her whole life, loves everyday adventures, cares for the environment and thinks that when a family works together in all areas, it creates a strong and happy bond where everyone feels valued and loved.

Email: jodi@intentionalmoney.com.au
Facebook: www.facebook.com/JPMoneyCoach
Website: www.intentionalmoney.com.au

Voices of Impact

Dori Stewart

If someone had told me that I would one day be called the Teacher Turned Entrepreneur, I would have laughed in their face. But here I am; my name is Dori Stewart, and I am a former high school STEM teacher who built a multi-million-dollar global brand.

My chemistry teacher, Mr Shoun, during high school, changed my life. Mr Shoun was one of the hardest teachers in the school, and his class was the most challenging class I took in high school. I went into the class scared, thinking there was no way I would pass. I believed I was terrible at science. But interestingly, he ended up being the first teacher that believed in me and pushed me to do my best. It was pivotal because passing that class made me feel smart for the first time in my life. It taught me that if I work hard and apply myself, I can achieve even the things I think are impossible. This experience made me want to become a teacher because I wanted to do the same for other students. I wanted to make others feel like they were smart. I wanted them to believe in themselves, that they too could do great things.

I taught engineering at the high school level for eleven years. Like most teachers, I loved teaching but was unhappy with my job. I was underpaid, burnt out, and constantly felt unappreciated. Without any support from the administration, it truly felt like I was drowning in dark waters. I got into teaching because I wanted to make a difference and impact lives, but it was almost like the system was designed to stop me from doing that.

Outside the classroom, I was also struggling in my personal life. You see, my husband and I were on rocky grounds. He often made me feel financially inadequate because, as a teacher, I didn't make enough money to be independent. As a result, I felt a financial imbalance in my marriage - I was miserable. I felt like I would not be able to leave and take care of my children on a teacher's salary. So, I stayed in the marriage and my job, even though they both made me unhappy and wanted to get out.

Throughout that time, I was the advisor of my school's Technology Student Association, an after-school Club where I would take my students to various competitions throughout the state and the nation. My students would compete against the best schools in different areas of science, technology, engineering, and math. This job was a volunteer gig that I did without pay on the weekends, during summers, and after school. Soon, I started bringing my kids, Kaley and Matthew, to these events.

That particular year, my high school students were to partake in a national competition in Orlando, Florida. I figured my kids would never forgive me if I went to the home of Disney and didn't take them. So, I decided to make a family trip out of it, and we did the whole Disney thing. Even though I had brought them to the theme parks, they were excited about the engineering competitions and wanted to compete too! Seeing how excited my

Voices of Impact

kids got at seeing what my high school students were doing was amazing. That moment made me think about ways to get my children excited about engineering.

Matthew was five, and Kaley was seven at the time. Kaley, my daughter, was starting to struggle with math in school. I wanted to show her that when you apply math, really cool things happen and that engineering is the application of math and science. Kids need to understand the difference between theory and practice. So I felt it was crucial to show kids real-world applications of what they were learning in their math and science classes. But they also need to know this as quickly as possible.

I felt that if we could introduce engineering to kids at a very young age and hook them in, show them how cool engineering was. Perhaps they would stick with it and ultimately apply for colleges in engineering programs and fill some of those engineering jobs of the future. Many girls I taught often say, "I wish I knew about this sooner. I would have started taking engineering classes earlier!" Some students felt it was too late for them and that they missed the boat on taking engineering classes in high school, which are required to get into a good engineering school. Unsurprisingly, women are underrepresented in STEM as we make up only about 28% of the workforce.

To my surprise, that upcoming fall, I got a flyer in my kids' backpack asking for parents who had a hobby or business and wanted to teach an after-school program for a fundraiser. So, I filled out the form, decided to teach an engineering class, and took what I was doing with my high school students. I switched it up to make it more developmentally appropriate for the elementary students and taught a civil engineering class. The response was fantastic! The kids had an absolute blast. Then, the parents started asking for more, so the principal asked me to come back, and I had someone pull me aside and say, "Hey, do you also offer summer camps?"

That was the beginning of a life-changing journey for me. I saw a business opportunity there and took it with both hands! Soon after, I started a company called Engineering for Kids, and this business practically blew up in my small town in Virginia.

Entrepreneurship...

My company, Engineering for Kids, offered more than just after-school programs, where I began offering summer camps. Birthday parties and programs for Boy Scouts and Girl Scouts. I was offering civil engineering, mechanical engineering, aerospace engineering, and many other engineering fields. I even added coding and robotics to the curriculum. I began expanding my programs to more than just elementary school students. I extended to pre-school and middle school students, offering the programs to kids between four and fourteen. At the end of that school year, I put in my resignation letter at my high school to run my company full-time.

This happened in 2008 during the great recession - one of the worst economic declines in US history and the housing market's collapse. To make matters worse, STEM was not yet a buzzword and was not exactly the juiciest product to sell. At least in my home state of Virginia, engineering was only taught in elementary schools to gifted and talented kids.

My friends and family thought I was nuts, and I didn't blame them. There I was, quitting my teaching job to start a company in a recession with zero business experience. And on top of that, I was going to teach engineering to 4 years olds? Remember, back then; most people had not yet heard of the acronym STEM, so quitting my job to run a STEM education company seemed rather dramatic. A business consultant told me point blank that my business idea would fail, but I ignored that too.

Gillian Tans said, "Starting a business is not for the faint of heart," I learned that the hard way. Going against the advice of friends, family, and experts took a lot of courage, but I did it anyway. I didn't know what would come of this path I was about to take, but I knew I had to try it. I had to do it for my sake and the sake of my kids.

To my surprise (and everyone else's), my business took off and started booming. Instead of spending money on sports camps, parents enrolled their kids in engineering camps. Parents had to spend their money wisely and felt that education was a good investment in their kids' futures. I started getting the interest of people from all over the world. People were asking if they could buy my curriculum or ask if I could bring the programs to their town. They found me by just Googling "engineering programs for kids."

This interest led me to begin looking for ways to grow my company outside my Virginia hometown. I knew that change was inevitable, and if I wanted my business to grow, I would have to embrace some changes. I decided that the franchising business model was the best way to grow my company. So I started doing the work! I took courses, read books, and spoke to consultants. I talked to anyone in the franchising industry that would give me their time. I earned my Certified Franchise Executive credentials from the International Franchise Association.

The hard work paid off, and I sold my first franchise in 2011. Ultimately, I grew my company to over a hundred and sixty-five locations in 35 countries over the next almost ten years, reaching over a million students. And in 2019, I received an offer to purchase my business from an Ed-Tech firm that I couldn't resist, and that deal closed in 2020.

To this day, I pinch myself all the time that I somehow could pull off that level of success, which has gotten me a lot of attention. I was interviewed for Forbes Magazine and featured in Kiplinger Magazine and the Wall Street Journal. I was a guest on live TV several times on networks like Fox Business and CNN Money. I was even listed as one of the Most Creative People in Business by Fast Company Magazine.

However, my entrepreneurial journey has not been a string of successes. My journey has been tested with many twists and turns along the way, but resilience has kept me going. Only my close family and friends know about my journey because I have had a few failed businesses in the past. I have put myself out there to all my friends and family and said, "Hey, I started this new business; please support me," only to fail at those businesses.

And even though I failed at those businesses, I think about a speech I heard from Brene Brown. She said, "I want to be in the arena. I want to be brave with my life. And when we make a choice to dare greatly, we sign up to get our asses kicked. We can choose courage, or we can choose comfort, but we can't have both. Not at the same time."

I like to think that I chose courage. When you think about starting a business, there might be self-doubt and even fear. But I have learned that courage is not the absence of fear. It is the ability to feel fear and still do it anyway. So I told myself it's okay to be scared, as long as I don't let the fear stop me.

Giving back...

Now that I have succeeded, I decided to give back to society, starting with women, who, like me, are teachers looking for more beyond the classroom.

I am so passionate about helping women, especially teachers, become entrepreneurs because this shift in my career has had the most significant impact on my life. If I had stayed in my teaching job, I would never have been able to reach over a million students. More than anything, I understand that making such a significant change in your career can be daunting. Teachers might even feel limited in their business options. But the truth is that there are so many options for teachers to start a business, and that is because teachers make natural entrepreneurs.

Teachers are trained problem solvers, and as you know, a good business solves a problem. Teachers are trained to be problem solvers; whatever specific entrepreneurial path they choose, this ability will be crucial to its success. All they need is the push to find that problem worth solving. Another reason why teachers make promising entrepreneurs is that they are passionate about learning. Nobody knows everything about something, and you must be open to learning to be a good entrepreneur. Teachers spend their entire time learning and teaching others to learn. Bringing that skill into entrepreneurship means they are available to adopt the best strategy for their business. Keeping your customers happy is another crucial part of entrepreneurship. Luckily, teachers are very good at serving people. They serve their students, their families, the school administration, and their community. They know how to meet the set standard and keep people satisfied, so transitioning into entrepreneurship is like stepping into another familiar territory.

Of course, not every teacher will become an entrepreneur, and there will always be a need for teachers in our society. But many teachers are underpaid and financially insecure. As a result, they experience burnout and do not receive enough support from the administration. They deserve better, and I would like to help them. Whether as a part-time job for additional income or a full-time career change, teachers who wish to become entrepreneurs need to know they can succeed. They need networks, resources, and, most importantly, they need support.

It has been two years now since I sold my company. This new chapter in my life is all about giving back. The first way I give back is with the Teacher Turned Entrepreneur podcast. Not only do I share my story on this podcast, but I also interview women who are successful entrepreneurs. I hope that my story and my guests' stories will leave my listeners inspired and ready to take action in their entrepreneurial journey.

My company, Dori Stewart Consulting, is the second way I give back. I believe everyone has a passion that can become a business, so I help teachers gain time and financial freedom through entrepreneurship. My coaching membership assists teachers worldwide in getting support and guidance from a teacher-turned-entrepreneur who has been in their shoes. Through my company, they also have support from fellow teachers starting businesses and resources for building and growing a business.

There's a quote from one of my favorite motivational speakers, Mel Robbins. She says, "Everything in your life is preparing you for something that hasn't happened yet." I find that message so powerful. My past has prepared me for my present, and even though the past wasn't rosy, there were hard lessons to be learned. Life gave me lemons, and I made some lemonade! My financial inadequacies and my desire for my independence fueled me to grow a successful business.

I feel very fortunate that I was able to get out of a bad marriage and take care of myself and my kids. When I look back at my crazy, winding entrepreneurial path, both the successes AND the failures. I believe it all led me to where I am supposed to be today. That place is to help other women on THEIR journey.

About the Author

From STEM teacher to building a multi-million-dollar, global brand, Dori Stewart has a wealth of knowledge and experience to share. She is a valuable resource for anyone looking to boost their own brand and dedicates her time to coaching others in the areas she has mastered after more than a decade of hard work.

Dori's journey began as a STEM teacher. She saw a need and came up with a solution. That idea became a business that she grew to more than 165 locations in 35 countries, reaching over 1 million students. She sold that business in 2020.

She has received numerous awards in recognition of her accomplishments. She was listed as one of The Most Creative People in Business by Fast Company Magazine. She has been featured on Fox Business, CNN Money, and in Forbes, Kiplinger Magazine, and the Wall Street Journal. Dori lives in Virginia with her husband and two children.

Email: hello@sheturnedentrepreneur.com
Website: www.sheturnedentrepreneur.com
Instagram: www.instagram.com/teacherturnedentrepreneur

Voices of Impact

Sharon L Bech

My spiritual journey has taught me that no matter what life serves us, 'We have a Choice'.

2015, My marriage was over, my mind was in a spin, and the loss of my home all seemed familiar.

My emotions were out of control; I could not breathe, the darkness was all around me, and it felt like a bad dream. I was so scared, the pain in my stomach hurt, and as I opened my eyes, the tears began to fall as I realise this is real and how it feels to be all alone.

It is the memory of that little girl who was taken away from her parents as a 5-year-old.

The overwhelming sadness started to take over, I knew I had to pull myself together, or I would go down a path of where I had been before, a place of darkness, a place I did not belong. I had the tools to get me out of this; being on a healing journey gave me tools to use in times like this; the lesson also taught me that I am never alone, for Spirit is always with me and will guide me home. It was time for me to remember...

I have a choice! I could sit in my sorrow, or I could choose to do something different.

I decided a new adventure was in need, and heading north to

Broome seemed to be a promising idea; a 2000km drive by myself was going to be another adventure I would never forget. It brought back memories of when I drove from Darwin to Broome back in 2006 when I turned up as a surprise for my sister's 40th birthday. The freedom of being on the open road, windows down, music blaring and singing like nobody's listening. Staying in caravan parks along the way and meeting new and interesting people, there was something about being on your own.

Arriving in Broome, the heat in the air, you knew you were up north, but I was glad to have arrived safe and was excited as my new adventure was about to begin; not that I knew what that meant, but I was excited all the same.

I settled in Broome and started working in the Tourist Information Centre; having worked in this field in Margaret River, it was like destiny had called me in. The season had just begun, and they were expecting a busy season, with over 1000 visitors in the centre a day, it sure tested your spirits, however having to experience the products we were selling to our visitors, known as a Famil, certainly made up for the exhaustion of the day.

After all that I had lost, I believed I had just gained, the experiences I had during the season were far beyond what I had ever imagined, and I had experienced adventures and places that some people only dream about.

It went so fast that before I knew it, the season was coming to an end; it only seemed like yesterday that I had arrived. I experienced so much on this journey and met some lovely people who are still good friends today. As the work is only seasonal, most of the staff return home either south or over east until the next season begins; it sounded like the perfect lifestyle. In the meantime, it was time for me to reconsider my options, as Broome was not the greatest place to be in the wet season, even if I was offered a permanent position.

Having been introduced to Facebook around this time, I thought it might be the place to find where to next. As I was scrolling one morning before work, I came across a post that made me sit up and take notice.

The post was, 'How to write a book in 48 hours; it certainly made me sit up and notice as it's something I had wanted to do for years and had been told on many occasions how my story inspired others. Being impatient as I am to write a book in 48 hours sounded a little too good to be true, but it intrigued me all the same, and I had to know more. I made contact, and after further discussion, I had to commit to a

4-day Retreat in Geelong where I would learn the steps to create my book, this really put a fire in my belly, and somehow, I knew this would lead me on another journey, and once again, I had to trust the guidance that I was receiving.

Whilst writing my book, I dared to dream a little, visualising myself on stage sharing my story, but my biggest dream was being on the couch with Oprah, I am her biggest fan and had watched her many interviews with people from all over the world sharing their stories. It was my dream to be that person one day. In 2010 Oprah came to Australia, and my only hope was for her to return.

2015 my book was published; it had taken 12 months to write, and what a journey it was, I faced writer's block, frustration, and shed many tears, but it was a journey I needed to go on to learn more about myself, to help me heal the corners of my heart that still held pain.

It taught me the many lessons it takes to succeed, perseverance being key, the belief in myself, to have patience and never letting go of the vision. I remember the day the boxes arrived, and I held my book in my hands for the first time; it was so surreal seeing it in its true form; the smell of something so new it brought up so many emotions, pride for believing in myself and all my hard work, the frustrations and tears I shed were worth it. I will never forget the happiness that bubbled up inside of me at that moment; I wanted to shout it from the rooftops; it was pure joy. I had succeeded in creating my story and could not wait to share it with the world.

The announcement that Oprah was returning to Australia gave me hope of fulfilling another part of my dream; however, I was to learn Oprah's visit to Australia was going to be different; this tour was about sharing her personal journey around Australia. I chose not to find out if she was inviting people on the stage, for it was easier than having to face the truth, the truth that I allowed fear to stop me.

That dream didn't stop me from wanting to share my achievement with my family, this book was also part of their journey, and I wanted to gift them with a copy to allow me to share some of their stories too. I was so excited and organised a family picnic. It was the day that my world once again came crashing down. My book was not well received.

I had dreamt of this moment sharing the excitement with my siblings, so their response came as a surprise. I felt hurt and all alone at that moment. That was the day that my books went under the bed to collect dust and were only discussed when the family were not around. I never allowed myself to celebrate or share my success with the world.

Once again, my message rang true "I have a choice."

As time went by, I never waived from my dreams and what I had envisaged for my future; I had to pick myself up and continue believing that one day my dream would come alive.

I did what I do best, headed back to Broome for the next tourist season, one where I would learn many lessons, one very valuable one, 'having expectations of others can often lead to disappointment.'

Over time I realised this book was my story, my success, not my siblings; it was wrong of me to expect the response I wanted, as that led to disappointment and the reason I put the books under the bed. The truth is, I was afraid to share my book with the world; I allowed my fear to take hold, and it was easier to create a story that kept me safe instead of sharing my success with the world.

It was the defining moment; my message in my book was ringing loud and clear, 'I have a choice.'

I decided at that moment to dust myself off and do something about it, I had the dream of creating my own business one day, and I needed to learn all I could to make it happen. The healing industry was something I wanted to pursue. I studied Reiki and Energy Healing and believed this was the direction I was to go in. I was ready to start a new and create the business of my dreams.

My book, Colourful Life, 'It's always Darkest before the Dawn' was now in our local Library and the two bookstores in town. I had been invited to share my story to a local woman's group, which was well received by sales and bookings for healing, the momentum had started, and I envisaged travelling further south to other regional towns offering to heal those in need and to share my story.

It was exhilarating, but every now and again, I would feel a wave of emotion, my stomach in knots; I knew it was the fear creeping in, but I was determined not to allow it to take hold this time, and I would have to ride this wave if I wanted to succeed.

And. then I received a call, a call that made me question it all. My previous work colleague asked me to return to Broome for the tourist season; I had not been back for two years and felt so good to be asked. I had to think long and hard about the decision, for I was 2 months into a 4-month housesit and pulling out did not feel right. My business was beginning to take shape, but deep down, I could not contain the excitement, the feelings one has the lead up to the season knowing how crazy it could be, but the exhilaration puts those thoughts to the back of your mind as you wonder what this season will bring, what experiences lay ahead and the people you meet, it made for a very tough decision, but one that had to be made.

As much as I loved having my own business, I created a story of all the reasons why it wasn't working or making enough money and that taking the job would be easier in the long run; it was the same excuses that I have told myself repeatedly so that I didn't have to be accountable for my actions.

I returned to Broome for the season and was offered a management role that gave me the leadership that I wanted; it also gave me the opportunity to travel further afield throughout the Kimberley's; however, over time, I realised what I had was more responsibility and not the freedom I was craving, the freedom to be my own boss and once again I began to search.

My search led me to Sydney, where I wanted to learn how to be a coach; even with my management and customer service skills and the ability to connect with people, I wanted to learn how to help others on a more personal level. I often have people come to me for advice. What I learnt was so profound, for it taught me that I had been doing it all wrong, that offering advice was not always the answer. A good coach guides the client through a process of questions that leads them to find their own answers. Offering advice was a skill I learned from a very young age as the mother to my siblings, but I needed to unlearn it if I wanted to be a good coach.

My journey is to continue to challenge myself, to never leave a stone unturned, and embrace the opportunities that are presented, for they help me grow and to become the better version of myself, even in those moments of despair, the ones that shake us to the core, those moments that wake us up to see the truth, and know it's time to do the work, to heal what is required for the journey ahead.

My fears have held me back for many years, and it was in those pivotal moments that I knew if I want a better life for myself, then it was up to me to make the changes. I do have a choice. It's a work in progress and one that never stops, and each day I continue to challenge myself to step out of my comfort zone. I remind myself of the skills I have gained through my own personal development and believe they are the gift I can share with others, and it gives me great joy when I see the results it can give to others.

One that will always stay with me is a Lady I met at a woman's circle, who was struggling with ideas around marketing for her business and asked me for some advice, I thought it was brave of her to reach out to someone she didn't know, but I was happy to assist, and organised a time to meet. That conversation made a huge difference to her business; with the advice I gave and the small changes required, her business has now gone on to the international market. It humbles me to see the results of something that I could be a part of.

When life gets tough, I feel privileged when I'm called upon by family members. It reaffirms that all I have learnt over the years can help others in need, even with family. It was shared recently that helping a family member who was struggling with life had made a huge difference, and I only hope they continue to reach out. The message from my book rang true, no matter what life serves us, 'we all have a choice', and that choice was theirs to make.

I am proud of who I have become; even with the fears that continue to lurk, it keeps me on my toes and continues to push me forward. Earlier this year, I decided to take some of my own advice and learn how to speak in public; it is the fear I need to overcome to share my story with the world. I joined a speaking group to learn the techniques, which are all about the breath. It's teaching me how to present my message to touch those who need it most, and with perseverance and consistency, it will give me the courage to stand on the stage or sit on the couch with Oprah. I believe my message will help hundreds, if not thousands, and it would be selfish of me not to share it.

My dream is to travel and share my message where it is needed and to make a difference, whether that is in group sessions, talking on podcasts, via webinars or speaking on stage or maybe I could create my own Oprah's couch and invite others to share their stories. However, I am not giving up on my Oprah dream; if I continue to dream, the magic may happen.

The dream of running my own business is still with me, and I trust that it will evolve over time. I would like to think that turning 60 next year will be a major turning point in my life. I don't believe stepping towards retirement is to quit life. It's a time to gather all the richness I have acquired over the years and share it with others. It's a time to create a Legacy for my children and grandchildren.

My future goal is to create a support network for women as I believe we are not meant to do this alone; I want to create a place to connect with like-minded women who are ready to step out of their comfort zone and are willing to do the work to create change for their future self. A place to share, learn and a place to encourage each other's growth and inspire one another on this journey called life!

As I close this chapter, I would like to share my message once more, a message that I believe needs to be shared with the world.

That no matter what difficulties we face in life, 'We have a Choice' in how we deal with them!

That choice can make all the difference in a moment!

About the Author

Sharon Bech is a published author who loves to travel; known as the gypsy in the family, her mission in life is to never leave a stone unturned; she believes life is for exploring to be challenged, and the life lessons we face are to teach us how to become a better version of ourselves.

Sharon's passion goes beyond the miles she has travelled, her knowledge and wisdom she has acquired, and a love of the Spirit world has given her the tools to help other like-minded women who don't want to do life alone, women who want to connect and learn how to overcome the challenges they face stepping into their later years! Sharon lives in Perth, Western Australia; her other interests are bushwalking, reading, crafts and catching up with family and friends. Her mission in this lifetime is to leave a Legacy for her children and grandchildren.

Email: sharonlbech@gmail.com
Facebook: www.facebook.com/sharon.bech.1763

Sharon's published book: Colourful Life, 'it's always Darkest before the Dawn.' (www.booklaunch.io/slbech/colourfullife)

Voices of Impact

Katie Chapman

Have you ever felt like a square peg in a round hole? When you feel like you should fit in, and you really try to fit in, but no matter how hard you try to fit in, you don't. How long did it take you to realise that there is nothing wrong with your shape but that the hole you're trying to fit into is not the right one for you? For me, it took about twenty years.

My life since childhood has been one crazy ride of chaos and spontaneity. The outward appearance of my childhood was of an English middle-class family, with my father a doctor, my mother a nurse, and me being the eldest of three children who were all popular and effortlessly academic. Behind closed doors, however, it was long working hours for my doctor dad and years of mental illness and long stays in mental hospitals with depression for my mum. This left me in a parental role at a young age, trying to look out for my brother and sister, whilst doing homework, cooking dinner, and never missing an episode of Neighbours or Home and Away. Growing up in southern England, this was my escape down under to an idyllic life in the sun in Australia.

Making it through my teenage years without getting arrested, achieving excellent grades at school, no major health and safety incidents, a few risky decisions leading to some incredible stories for my kids, and jobs at prestigious companies including IBM and Porsche, I eventually found my way to university and achieved a BSc (Hons) in Applied Psychology and Computing.

When it was time to look for a graduate job, I had friends in London earning an astronomical amount of money in recruitment. As my dissertation had been HR-focused, studying the effect of the interview medium on interview performance and satisfaction, I figured this would be the industry for me! I just hadn't realised recruitment was a sales role when my focus was very much on aligning people's strengths and characteristics with finding the right role for them, not how quickly I could get ANYONE into ANY ROLE as long as they had the right skills and the clients paid the bills.

Temp recruitment in London was cutthroat with very long hours, and the active social life that came with the job made the hours even longer! After nine months, I questioned my career decision. Although I loved London and had some great friends there, something was missing, and it didn't feel right. Dressing in suits made me feel like I was 'playing dress ups', and I felt stupid in client meetings as I didn't know what to say and, quite frankly, didn't really care about what they told me.

At that point, I decided to go on holiday to Australia to see a friend I had met at IBM when she was travelling many years ago. This was the first milestone moment in my life. By the end of the short trip from Sydney airport to Maroubra beach, where my friend lived, I had gone from not wanting to come here to being completely sold on the country. My neighbours and Home and Away moments were here! I holidayed up and down the east coast from Sydney to the Whitsundays and back, having an interview with a large recruitment firm before I flew home. With a business sponsorship visa, my belongings packed, London Marathon done, and goodbyes said, I moved to Australia within a few months of returning from my holiday. Spontaneous, risky, fun.

Australia was a breath of fresh air compared to London. Recruitment was easy and fun; clients wanted to drink coffee with you and talk about their lives, not just work, and everyone was polite. The sun was shining, the beaches were amazing, and everything felt so clean. My parents said I sounded completely different on the phone. I was confident and calm, not like I had been in London when I was stressed and anxious. I relocated to Brisbane eighteen months after I landed in Australia and continued to work in recruitment, moving into internal recruitment and HR with a top-tier professional services firm and ASX-listed IT consulting firms after I had my children.

When working in these organisations, I realised what had drawn me to recruitment all those years before, when deciding on my dissertation topic at university and subsequently taking the recruitment role in London. It was the alignment of values. Not skills and experience but the values of individuals aligning with the organisation's values to create a synergy beyond the technical and professional competencies. Ultimately, these can be taught. But can you teach someone to change their belief system and what drivers are important to them? No.

You can't train someone to be a different person, and you can't change yourself to fit into a job.

Whilst I was still 'playing dress-ups' and feeling silly in meetings, at least I was now doing work I valued, and I could see the tangible outcomes my work achieved for others.

The importance of values in career and hiring decisions remained central to how I operated in my corporate roles and in my own resume writing and career coaching business that I established as a single mum when my children were young. Guiding people in their career choices and understanding more about themselves beyond their skill set enabled me to support my own values of empowering others and freedom of time, as I could work my business around my children. I worked with a wide range of clients from various industries and professional backgrounds, but I gained the most satisfaction from working with women who didn't believe they had anything significant to offer. By using my VIBES method (Values, Intuition, Beliefs, Empowerment, Strengths), we uncovered their values, what they enjoyed and what they were great at, aligning these with opportunities and areas to explore, so they could see what jobs and organisations they aligned with. Seeing their confidence grow by believing what they were capable of was amazing.

Whilst the business was successful, I returned to the corporate world to take on a challenging and exciting role in a new HR/Recruitment function to build this into a values-based recruitment function supporting a national organisation. Just as it did in my resume writing business, I soon became aware of how amplifying women's strengths and supporting their values improved their confidence and self-belief when they often felt 'less than'. I was working in a very male-dominated industry, and when an opportunity presented itself to join a boutique consultancy to lead their talent strategy in an industry that supported the empowerment of women, I took it. The people I worked with were inspiring, and the role was challenging. Then Covid happened.

When you are at the start of a global pandemic with no idea where it will lead, and there is a global sense of fear, what better time to quit your job? (Did I mention I make spontaneous, risky decisions?!) The world felt like it was about to descend into chaos, the expectations of my role were suddenly changing in a direction I didn't align with, whilst my working hours were being reduced to avoid redundancy. I didn't take this decision lightly and consulted with a mentor I valued highly, but I knew what I needed to do. I was out of alignment with what was important to me, where my strengths were and how I wanted to show up. Leaving was my only option. So, I did.

I knew I could fall back on my resume writing business, but I also knew this was ultimately not what I wanted to do. I decided to go back to studying psychology and commenced online studying. It was during this period that my personal self-awareness was increasing. Without the stifling corporate jacket that I had been wearing for so many years, I began to notice things like how I could sit down at my laptop at 9 am and still not have done anything by 3 pm. How I could begin one task and then realise I was in the middle of three different, unrelated tasks. Or how I would suddenly have to leave the office and walk around the house or go for a drive for a change of scenery. After watching a few TikTok videos sent from my son, with messages saying 'this is you, mum' or 'you do this all the time!', a conversation with my GP and a referral to a psychiatrist, I was diagnosed with ADHD-combined type at the age of 43.

To say this was life-changing was an understatement. Not only did I now understand why I did certain things (risky behaviour, impulsive decisions, talking way too much for some people), but I also understood why I found it so hard to do things that other people find so easy (be on time, be organised, remember things, move from thought to action) and why I have so many ideas but rarely get them off the ground (thanks hyperactive brain!). I also learnt about 'chasing dopamine' and why completing things can be so hard. With a combination of medication and therapy, I am now adapting my life to suit my brain (square peg, square hole) rather than forcing myself to fit in the wrong-shaped hole. Even with the treatment, my neurodivergent brain will not be the same as a neurotypical brain, but that's ok. Wouldn't the world be boring if we were all the same!

Since my dramatic corporate exodus, personal and professional re-evaluation and ADHD diagnosis, my life has fallen into place. Whilst I enjoy a challenge, I no longer seek out chaos purely for dopamine. I can make considered assessments about my situation. I have gained clarity on my direction and can now take action to make things happen, and I am helping other women make values-aligned choices that enable them to live and work in ways they believe in and feel fun and easy for them. The key to all of this? Aligning values and action.

So, what are your personal values? You may have a clear answer to this, but you may still struggle with the concept of what values are. Think of yourself as a ship, and life is the journey. Your values are the compass that steers you in the right direction. They are the beliefs you have that influence your choices and behaviours. Some values will remain consistent throughout your life; others will change as your life evolves and what is most important to you changes. My values as a single 26-year-old who just arrived in Australia were different to now, being a wife, mum of two and a business owner. For example, 'find the fun in what you do' has been a consistent value for me as I believe we can always have fun, whereas my wild adventure-related values have toned down, and family-related values have a higher priority.

When you understand your values, you will understand how aligning what you do with what is most important to you will feel easy and fun. When you are out of alignment with your values and are living and working in a way that does not match your beliefs, it can feel hard; you can experience imposter syndrome and feel inauthentic in what you do. Like a square peg in a round hole.

Think about something in your life; it could be your job, your home life, a hobby/ activity or your relationship. Now think about how it makes you feel. Do you get excited when you think about it, or do you feel bored or anxious? Is it the whole thing that makes you feel that way, or just a part of it? When you break it down and become aware of your feelings, you can see whether it supports your values or not. Take exercise, for example. If you value health and fitness, it will be important to you. When I think about exercise classes, I feel stifled and bored, but when I think about running, I feel energised and motivated. Both are exercises, but only one appeals to me. The reason is that another core value of mine is freedom of time. I value having the freedom to do what I want when I feel like it, not when it is scheduled. This is also a common factor with ADHD; planning or committing to something in advance than not feeling like doing it when the time comes around! I love running because I can do it whenever I feel like it. It is free and not scheduled, so if I plan to go for a run in the evening but don't feel like it when the evening comes around, I can go the next morning. I still do the exercise and meet that value, but I do it when it suits me, so I also meet my value of time freedom. If I had to go to the exercise class, it would feel hard and unenjoyable for me. What do you do that supports your values?

One particular client of mine was in marketing and was incredibly unfulfilled in her job. Despite recommending new ideas and ways to improve their outcomes, she wasn't listened to and felt stifled and stuck. When I met her, she dreamed of combining her law degree and marketing experience in a very specific role but didn't believe she was capable based on her current employer's lack of interest in her. She lacked confidence in what she had to offer and was frustrated as she couldn't see a way to do what she loved. By using my VIBES method, we increased her awareness of her value, improved her confidence, focused on her strengths, and created a targeted plan to apply for her dream position. She got the position, and her new employers said her application was the best they had ever seen. Her value was clear, her alignment with the role was perfect, and her confidence skyrocketed as she felt appreciated for what she had to offer.

A psychologist I have had the pleasure of working with had found herself at odds with the profession she loved as she was feeling emotionally and physically burnt out with no time for herself to recuperate. As a single mother with a young autistic son, the demands of her job in private practice were becoming too much. Knowing her passion for helping people and her vocation to effect tangible change in people's lives, it was a sign to do some work together when she started searching for part-time administration roles that would never give her the professional satisfaction she needed. We broke down her current home and work situations to see what was missing that she needed and what wasn't serving her. We uncovered her values, with her highest values being psychological safety and professional learning. With her time and energy being stretched between her home and work life, she didn't feel aligned with either of these. She felt frustrated, exhausted and drained and that she was letting everyone down. Once we identified that reallocating some of her time to more fulfilling activities was key, she found a work-from-home telehealth position, providing mental health triage to various patients. This allowed her to manage her time more efficiently and to provide her son with the focused support he needed and she valued. She continued her professional development and engagement with clients and peers with less impact on her time. By adjusting her circumstances to meet her values, she felt calmer, more fulfilled, and less stressed in her role and confident that she was providing the quality time and attention her son required.

I love seeing the lightbulb moment when women realise their value and what they have to offer, and that they really can have an easier and more fulfilling life when they engage with what is most important to them rather than focusing on what is important to others. Our values are our compass, so let them guide you!

What would you like to change in your life? Are you like me, chaotically carefree and need a business/ job/ life that stops you from feeling stifled and engages your passion and creativity? Or are you like my psychologist client and want a structure that works for you in your professional and personal life to keep order and safety? When we are living and working in our flow, the people we support are able to better support people in their lives because of the benefit they receive from us.

My purpose is to help as many women as possible to realise their values, align their values with actions and have the confidence to share their unique strengths with the world; taking women from frustrated, stifled and insecure to calm, confident, energised when they are in flow with what's important to them.

Are you ready to share your value and find a path that leads you to what is most important to you, aligning your values, choices and actions? I would love to see you in my Facebook group (@calmvibesoultribe), where I will share my upcoming courses and how you can work with me to achieve fun and fulfilment in an easy and calm way.

The more empowered women we have engaging with each other, the more our impact will be seen in our generation and future generations. My vision of guiding as many women as possible to confidently live their values, share them, and empower them to do what feels right for them, starts here.

I hope this is the start of your journey to values-aligned confident choices and an empowered life you will love!

About the Author

After an extensive career in HR and Talent focused on developing values-based strategies and processes, Katie's business, Calista & Co, now guides women to uncover their values and align their lives with what is most important to them, transforming feelings of boredom, frustration, and struggle to confidence, empowerment, and fun!

Katie's intuitive ability to identify others' values and strengths enable her to guide her clients on their journey to understanding themselves on a deeper level and leading a more aligned, authentic and fulfilling life, achieving dreams and new levels of success. Katie is an advocate for women with ADHD (and the chaotically carefree!), having been diagnosed herself in her 40's. She is passionate about exploring the connection between values, ADHD, and following your own path to support sustainable success in careers, business, relationships, and life, with maintained feelings of confidence and fun.

Instagram: www.instagram.com/calista_and_co
Website: www.calistaandco.com

Dr Carolyn Daniels

Heart Search

I believe as a woman; you have an intrinsic ability to harness your potential, empower other women on their journey of personal growth and make a difference in your own and others' lives. I can say without a doubt that I know you can achieve your hopes, wishes and long-lost dreams. I know you can overcome self-limiting thought patterns and the overwhelm caused by issues such as imposter syndrome. I know this because I have.

As part of my alignment with these beliefs, I want to share some of my journey with you and hope it encourages you to embrace your potential and claim your destiny.

I was forty-seven when my second marriage broke up. I was lost and broken, it was just another disaster to add to the already long list, but out of the heartache, past hopes and dreams began to emerge. One of these long-held dreams I thought impossible to achieve was going to university.

I was encouraged to enrol by several women, including my sister, who nagged me, *"You should've gone to uni when you left school. Now's your chance, just go."*

When I went to Centrelink to ask about study support, the

woman I spoke with said, *"I see lots of women like you, very capable with lots of skills and no qualifications. Take this opportunity now, go to university."*

I ended up going to university, but the main reason was to learn to write. I wanted to write a book, to get it out of my heart space. And with that book, I wanted to encourage women to be overcomers.

I graduated with Distinction and started work at the university. I immediately enrolled in an Honours degree, knowing full well that the year was going to be difficult. I was working full-time, my partner at the time had cancer, and my son Jack qualified to ride in the High School Rodeo Finals in America. My daughter Bianca and I fundraised for Jack, I got a large credit card, and we headed off to America halfway through my Honours year.

At the end of that year, my partner died. Grief took a huge toll on my energy and endurance. While I graduated with my Honours degree, it took time to heal from the combination of heartbreak and study pressures.

Broken Heart

I did learn to write at university, and I did write a book. It is a memoir, my personal story that I hoped would inspire women to break free from the self-limiting inner critic, to open the door to their courageous, authentic selves and to bring their hopes and dreams to fruition.

My story highlights a dark period in Australia's history, a social record of shame and exclusion. I want to share this story in the hope that it inspires you to reach your goals, especially those who may be struggling with past traumas or unfulfilled ambitions.

I was pregnant at fifteen. Too terrified to tell Mum, I agonised for several months about how to tell her. At four months pregnant, there was nowhere to hide. Eventually, I had to let her know. But how to find the words? Mum was furious and horrified. She worked as a midwife at the local hospital and wanted me to have an abortion, but it was too late by then. From that time on, I was virtually imprisoned at home.

I had a beautiful baby girl who I was allowed to see once but not allowed to touch. She looked like an Indian Princess sleeping in the plastic hospital bassinet. That image burned into my brain forever.

I went back to school, and it wasn't spoken of again. I suffered post-traumatic stress, started drinking, survived a violent relationship and struggled through the years to deal with the loss and pain. I shifted around a lot, then married for a second time. I lived out west in Central Queensland, the wife of a fencing contractor. We had two beautiful children, but the image of the little girl I gave up haunted my quiet times. Was she okay? Was she still alive? What were her parents like? And every year on her birthday was pure agony.

My husband lived the life of a single man who happened to be married. Drunk again, he lay next to me, snoring in bed. Sighing, I picked up the book I had purchased earlier that day. It told the story of an abused young woman who had her baby forcibly removed. Shell-shocked at the similarity, it felt like I was hurtling to the ground from a great height. Anguished sobs tore the air. I couldn't breathe. This was the trigger I was too terrified to look for. The trigger that let me know it was time to search for my little dark-haired girl. That little girl would now be twenty-one years old.

I knew there was an adoption helpline in the telephone book. Every relinquishing mother knows it. I sat by the phone trying to collect myself before dialling the number. When a woman answered my call, I started crying. I cried so hard I had trouble breathing, and I couldn't speak to the person on the other end of the line. It took three calls over a week to make myself understood and so began the process to find my daughter.

The steps involved in contact took many months. I had a telephone interview with a counsellor from the Adoptive Information Service. Eventually, they forwarded a letter to me. I nervously opened the thick letter that included the adoption paperwork. I fumbled through the documents and saw that my daughter had been named Karen by her parents. She had turned twenty-two by now. I could also see documents from Family Welfare that assessed Mum's role in the adoption process and a roundup of what they thought of me. My stomach rolled when I read their appraisals written twenty-two years earlier. Item 5 detailed Mum's reaction to my 'predicament'. Item 6 was a brief assessment of my 'reaction to pregnancy, intelligence, personality, interests, etc.' I felt like an observer to a past experiment.

I was instructed to write a letter to Karen. It was forwarded to her by the Department of Human Services. I checked our Post Office box every day, waiting, wondering if I would get a reply. Weeks later, an envelope arrived that I thought could be special. I drove straight home, and ran up the crumbling brick steps into the kitchen, throwing the assorted mail on the table. All except the special letter. I sat down quickly, breathing harder now. With shaking hands, I carefully tore the envelope open and pulled out a handwritten letter. My heart pounded against my rib cage as I hurriedly looked for the signature at the end of the letter. In handwriting similar to mine it said, 'Love from Karen.'

Enclosed in the letter was her photo. I held it up to the light with shaking hands. Primal groans fell out of my mouth as I examined the photograph. Tears of joy, disbelief and wonder poured down my face as I looked upon the face of the most beautiful young woman smiling out of the photo. I put my head on the table and cried. Great heaving sobs.

Karen was keen to meet me. The letter included her phone number to arrange our meeting. Letters were one thing, but to talk directly to Karen took all the courage I could muster. I sat and looked at the telephone, trying to pull myself together to make the call. With shaking hands and a quaking heart, I took a deep breath, picked up the phone and dialled the number.

What an epic phone call. *"Hello Karen, this is Carolyn speaking,"* I said, sounding much calmer than I felt.

"Oh, hello Carolyn, it's so nice to hear your voice." She sounded lovely. I'm sure I sounded like a nervous wreck. My stomach rolled, tears were bashing at the back of my eyeballs, my heart was exploding in my chest, and all the while, I tried to sound normal. *"I can't wait to meet you,"* Karen's pleasant voice said on the other end of the line.

"I can't wait either," I answered. I got off the phone, overcome with feelings that I had trouble describing. How does a heart burst yet still stay intact?

Why I organised to meet at a service station halfway between the 300 kilometres that separated us I'll never know, but thinking had actually become difficult, and that's where Karen and I would meet for the first time since I'd peered into that plastic hospital bassinette twenty-two years earlier.

Heart Healing

I bought a new red dress for the day. A thousand splattered thoughts twisted through my head as I drove to our meeting place. Arriving early, I sat outside at a table flicking through a magazine and kept an eye on the service station driveway. The normal humdrum of life flowed on around me as my life rewound to that lonely place twenty-two years earlier.

A little purple car whizzed into the service station, and I knew from the photo Karen had included in her letter that it was her.

My heart pounded wildly, and I held my breath as I waited for her to get out of the car and walk over. I stood to greet her. A thousand racing emotions sped through my flesh.

"Hello Karen," I said, opening my arms wide. And I held my girl in my arms for the first time ever. I felt bands of searing pain snap off my heart. I was set free, and I could feel it happening inside. How do you explain doves flying out of your heart? How do I explain freedom? What does it look like? How do I describe the countless number of tears I'd cried finally being answered? How do you peel back half a lifetime of shame? Freedom is as close as I can get. I kept my tears under control. I just wanted to savour this experience. Every wondrous moment.

"*It's so lovely to meet you at last,*" Karen said. We sat down and talked about anything and everything. It felt so right and natural.

"*My family calls me Cazz,*" Karen told me. My heart rolled in my chest.

"*My family call me Cazz, too,*" I said, incredulous. What serendipity to have the same nicknames. The natural, unseen world has unexplained connections to us all and this was one more example of the ties that link us together.

After an unbelievable afternoon of sharing stories and memories, I drove home full of feelings and emotions that I hadn't experienced before. Enormous, beautiful feelings welled up inside me. I felt lighter, freer, joyous, and happy and every other feel-good word I could recall. The secret pain I'd carried in my heart for twenty-two years was no longer there. I reflected on *why the big secret, why the hidden heartbreak?* Now I knew the answer. Shame keeps us shackled. The darkness that surrounds secrets creates silent pockets of a life half lived. And today I was free.

Bold Heart

When writing my book, I researched Prime Minister Julie Gillard's apology for forced adoptions that she delivered on the 13 March 2013. As a prelude to the apology, a Senate investigation found 'evidence that social conditions in the 1950s, 60s and 70s were hostile to unmarried mothers' (The Senate 2012, p. 39). These young unmarried mothers, deterred by governments and religious institutions from keeping their babies, suffered collectively, stigmatised as 'sluts'.

In 2013, Hon Julia Gillard, then Prime Minister, issued an apology to those impacted by forced adoption, acknowledging the 'mothers who were betrayed by a system that gave [them] no choice and subjected [them] to manipulation, mistreatment, and malpractice ...' (Australian Government 2013). From the 1950s, 60s and 70s an estimated 150,000 unwed mothers had their babies forcibly removed. This practice was carried out and approved of by governments, churches, hospitals, charities, and bureaucrats. And I can add families too.

Most of these relinquishing mothers, their children, and their families are still alive today. This past ill-treatment was written into the laws of our nation and has reached forward, resulting in impacts that still cut across the generations today.

Finding Heart

My thought life was a mess after I had Karen. Over the years, I worked on my inner life to try to find peace and balance. I read every self-help book I came across and listened to motivational videos and podcasts. In my late twenties, I had a spiritual encounter after a particularly heartbreaking episode with my second husband. I left him for a while, ending up back home at Mum's place. Lonely and broken, one night, I scanned the bookshelf for a topic that might distract me. I can't remember the name of the book, but it had a New Age focus.

The book had all my philosophies on life and death, that our spirit lives on after death, that unseen beings watch over us, and that our lives are connected and relevant in the greater theme of life. That no experience in our lives is wasted. The final chapter mentioned something about God, and it all gelled for me. I put the book down, and said, "I believe," and with that was immobilised. I knew it was a God-thing and all I could think was *this is better than drugs and grog*. I was being regenerated from the inside out. I was filled with what I can only describe as love. Joyous feelings rippled up and down the sinews and tendons holding my body together.

While I was a believer after this experience, I still drank and smoked, and life at that time didn't get any easier. I just had an inner strength and knowledge that came from beyond myself.

Over the ensuing years, I drew on this strength to give up smoking and drinking, to find the courage to look for my adopted daughter, and to forge pathways to inner healing. Wherever I lived, I had a supportive network through women's groups. I was supported, I supported others, and I always pursued internal relief from painful memories and whatever drama was going on in my life at the time. This combination of belief in a power beyond our human experience, hope for a better life, and, when the opportunity presented, choosing further education to help achieve my dreams gave me insight, resilience, and, ultimately, a journey from darkness to light.

Strong Hearts

As part of this growing strength, I completed a PhD. My study explored how Australian women navigate the transitions to higher education and the workforce. Many of the women experienced power inequity in workplaces and households, including domestic violence for some. While educational and workplace opportunities have improved for Australian women, workplace discrimination, work/life balance, childcare, equal pay and paid parental leave remain problematic for many.

The marginalisation and silencing of women are well documented, but the system changes required are slow. One relevant example is the decades it took to amend adoption policies in Australia. These legislated policies were built on the 'clean break theory' of removing babies from their mothers as soon as possible to allegedly protect the baby's welfare and spare the mother the 'disgrace of single motherhood' (The Senate 2012, p. 12). What we need is systemic change where equality for women is the norm. We need to continue to confront the injustices written into the systems that govern us and call for structural and systemic change.

Reflecting on my life experience, I know encouragement for women's empowerment, confidence building, and resilience is necessary; however, this will not change the current status quo. Only our combined voices will.

In spite of all this, I absolutely believe that you can do whatever it is your put your mind to. I know if you have a clear goal that you look at it every morning when you wake up, that you can achieve it. I know you can overcome past trauma and live fulfilling lives, achieving your hopes and dreams. I know this can be true for you because it was true for me despite the heartache and roadblocks I encountered along the way. Challenges can impact our lives, but having goals helps to keep us on track.

Sharing Strength

My story is the story of tens of thousands of relinquishing mothers across the 1950s, 60s and 70s in Australia. Whenever I have the opportunity to share my story, invariably, someone will say, *"You too"*. What they mean is they, too, are relinquishing mothers, or they know someone who is.

So, how am I going to keep making a noise about women's issues? Through my writing. I will work on finally getting my book published. I will talk about it wherever I am invited and keep writing and making a noise to call out injustice and inequity.

I want to thank you for reading my story. I hope that you have been inspired to follow your dreams, seek your destiny, and believe you can achieve all that is written in your heart.

Whatever your life story may be, my wish for you is authenticity, courage, freedom, and, if required, the gift of inner healing on your journey through this precious life.

If you need someone to talk to after reading this story, you can reach out to one of the following helplines:

Forced Adoption Support Services: 1800 21 03 13

Beyond Blue: 1300 22 4636

Lifeline: 13 11 14

Mensline: 1300 789 978

Relationships Australia: 1300 364 277

And if you haven't been told this today, know that I think you are amazing.

References:

Australian Government 2013, *National Apology for forced adoptions*, https://www.ag.gov.au/families-and-marriage/national-apology-forced-adoptions

The Senate Community Affairs References Committee [The Senate] 2012, *Commonwealth contribution to former forced adoption, policies and practices*, Community Affairs Reference Committee, February 2012, Commonwealth of Australia, Canberra, ACT.

About the Author

Born in the Wimmera Mallee town of Horsham, Carolyn has lived and worked in most states of Australia.

After a turbulent young life and two failed marriages, Carolyn finally enrolled in university as a mature age student. She honed her writing skills, aiming to empower women to face their fears and be overcomers.

A recent PhD graduate, Carolyn is a published academic author, regularly presenting at national and international conferences. Recently nominated for *Regional Women's Network Central Queensland* Inspirational Woman of the Year, Carolyn is passionate about women having a voice.

She enjoys early morning walks along the unspoiled beaches of the Capricorn coast or sitting at a beach-side café watching the moon rise over the balmy waters. When she isn't working, Carolyn and her partner Gary can be found renovating their seaside cottage or dancing up a storm at a local blues bar.

Email: carolyn.daniels0213@gmail.com

Najma Khan

"Every answer you are looking for is always found deep within you. Never comes from the head, always from the heart …." ~Najma Khan

"Mummy, for my birthday, can I get a water well built too?" was a question posed by my 8-year-old.

I didn't realise at the time that he was absorbing everything from an interview I was listening to. It was Marie Forleo interviewing Scott Harrison, the Founder of Charity Water. My son at the time decided that instead of having a birthday party and gifts, he would instead help others in Africa by giving them the gift of water. This is where it all began.

Why?

I had started my business just 6 months earlier as I was slowly becoming bored of being a stay-at-home mum. My why was to help as many young girls as possible in developing countries get an education, but I didn't really have it all figured out yet. This was exactly how it was going to be possible. Yes, I build as many water wells as possible from the profits I made from my business. Building these water wells would not just provide clean drinking water to families but would give many young children the opportunity to go to school and get the education they so desired rather than waste hours every day carrying water between source and village.

I was born in South Africa at a time when the effects of apartheid touched every aspect of daily life. Apartheid was a system built on many decades of official racial discrimination in South Africa and entrenched racially-based discriminatory legislation on the statute books since the late 1940s. It was designed to keep people of differing ethnic backgrounds separate in all avenues of life.

Despite this, I was fortunate to be born into and raised by parents who did everything to provide their children with the best education and raise us to be to become confident and focused individuals.

For my parents to make this possible and to fulfil this obligation, the one way to do it was to start a business. My parents were creative and started a clothing manufacturing business where they made corporate and school wear. My parents did the typical things all business owners tend to do work hard and spend most, if not all, your time building your business. Despite all the official and personal discrimination and prejudice encountered, they were able to build a great business through hard work, long hours and perseverance.

In the early 1990s, things were changing for South Africa, and in 1994 apartheid laws were officially abolished. Unfortunately for those of us born during the apartheid era, we were saturated with the belief that we were never good enough, sadly because of the colour of our skin. Nonetheless, the country had elected its first non-white president, and things were slowly changing.

Because of these changes, businesses were given many opportunities, and one very interesting opportunity that arose for our family business was a contract that I had managed to secure with a government department. Unbeknown to me at the time, this included designing and manufacturing uniforms for the State President's Residence staff in my home city.

Meeting The President

It's been said that there are at least ten things you should do in your life before you leave this world, and one of those things is to meet an important person. For me, this was meeting the first non-white President of South Africa, Nelson Mandela. Can you imagine my joy and jubilation the day I met President Nelson Mandela? Yes! I was over the moon, and I was also handed a bouquet of flowers. We spoke about "Invictus", a poem by William Ernest Henley that he recited frequently during his imprisonment, and the two lines in the poem that inspired him daily:

> *"I am the master of my fate; I am the captain of my soul"*

My biggest takeaway from the very short conversation I had with South Africa's First Black President was:

> *Always call out injustice, even when we see it in ourselves. Greatness lies within all of us.*

Although things seemed to be changing in South Africa, the crime rate was slowly increasing, and as we were in business, we were an easy target. I personally had gone through the trauma of being held at gunpoint in our business (an experience I do not wish upon anyone or would like to remember). This was a turning point for me, and it was now time to reconsider and decide if always living in fear was truly a way of life. Sadly, South Africa has never really recovered from criminality, and things seem to be getting worse.

I am grateful that I decided to leave and choose a safer place.

Coming to Australia

"Touchdown" and welcome to Australia. A place to call home where I knew no one, had no contacts and didn't even have a clue what to do. Coming to a new country and leaving behind all the comforts I was so used to was not an easy decision, but this was what I had chosen, and I was going to give it my all.

I love numbers, so I was naturally drawn to apply for a position in a bank. After going through a multitude of aptitude tests, I was accepted and worked for two of the big four banks in Australia. It was not long before I applied to work for a company that was very similar to my parent's business. I loved what I did and enjoyed working, but something within me felt unfulfilled. Becoming a mum was my passport to leaving the workforce, and I haven't looked back since.

I was now a full-time mum to my son, and my decision to home-school him from day one allowed me to be available for my family and start researching what I truly was called to do.

By July 2014, I had started a bookkeeping business, but it wasn't just any business: it needed to revolve around my lifestyle, make a profit and allow me to fulfil my dream to help as many young girls as possible in developing countries get an education. As a young child, I watched my parents work long hours in their business, which was not what I wanted to replicate. In all my research on starting a business, there was always one word that appeared time and time again, and that word was 'CLARITY'. Getting clear on what it is you personally want and what you want for your business was crucial, and this clarity has been helping me slowly tick off the goals that I want to be fulfilled.

Profit is a Habit, not an Event
~ Mike Michalowicz

Being a numbers person, I was drawn to a book written by Mike Micahlowicz titled *Profit First*, which he had just self-published in 2014, a few months before I started my business. I read the book with great interest, and the system he wrote about resonated with me as it was very similar to the envelope system my mum used with paying suppliers in their business. I implemented this system effortlessly in my own business from the very start, and not only was I able to run my business around my lifestyle, but I was able to build my first water well with the profits I made in my business.

Within the first six months of implementing this cash flow methodology and seeing the results I was getting in my own business, I was convinced that if I shared this with my clients, they, too, could become sustainably profitable. I did not hesitate to contact Mike Michalowicz and his team in the United States and asked if this was something I could do with my clients.

I was ecstatic when I was told that they were certifying accountants, bookkeepers, and coaches in this methodology. My gut instinct was to immediately sign up and start the certification process, and I was one of the very first Profit First Professionals in Australia to become certified.

Becoming certified allowed me to fully support my clients with all the tools, knowledge and, most importantly, the experience of guiding my clients through the Profit First journey.

The phrase *Profit First* is exactly what it is; it is that simple. As a business owner, the profit you make is yours, and yours alone, so taking it first is exactly what you should be doing. This is the reason why you started your business, right? Surely no one starts a business to make a loss.

In Profit First, we alter the accounting equation. Instead of the traditional equation:

Revenue − Expenses = Profit, we use the Profit First equation:

Revenue − Profit = Expenses.

We prioritise profit. We literally take our profit first!

In Profit First, we work with our natural biological and physiological makeup. We own up to Parkinson's Law. Rather than operate from a scarcity mindset, we create an illusion of scarcity. We do this via the use of bank accounts.

With Profit First, you open bank accounts, lots of them. These bank accounts act as digital envelopes. Each account is appropriately named.

Each bank account has a purpose. These bank accounts ensure our profitability. With Profit First, all income is collected within a single bank account; we transfer money from the income account to several other bank accounts based upon pre-designated percentages. By implementing this cash management system, we can immediately determine what amounts go toward salary, tax reserves and profit.

This is where I come in. As a Profit First Professional I help my clients determine the percentage they should be transferred into these accounts. But it is not just about determining percentages; it is much more than that.

Bank account accounting is how most business owners make spending decisions. For example, when an exciting new course or software comes out, most small business owners will simply check their bank account balance to determine whether they should buy it. Our buying decision is based on the amount of money we have in our bank account. We will say either, "Yes, we have the funds; let's do this," or, "Well, maybe not today." By having separate accounts, everything becomes so much clearer. We now become intentional; we know exactly what the money is set aside for.

When I became certified in the Profit First system, I knew I would be helping my clients generate profits, manage cash flow, establish boundaries, and really get them to understand their money habits.

It's Not Your Fault

To expand this journey, I am happy to share with permission the experience of the founder of *Speaking Styles* and *Voices of Impact*, Melanie Wood.

Melanie was already running her business for five years, but when it came to the finance side of things, she so eloquently said, "I have no idea what I'm doing". Melanie was driven, passionate and focused on helping others, that she really did not pay attention to the numbers in her business.

Melanie reached out to me as one of her goals was to reach the GST threshold.

Everything looked great as far as the accounting software was concerned, but when we looked deeper at the 'books', there was confusion. The number one cardinal mistake most start-ups make is running both business and personal finances from one account, and this is exactly how Melanie was running her business. This was something that had to be fixed immediately. Doing this gave Melanie clarity, and she could attain her first goal, which was to become GST-registered within a very short period.

We really needed to determine if the business was profitable, and by separating the business finances from the personal finances, we could determine this easily.

Another big goal Melanie wanted to be fulfilled was to buy her own home, and within fourteen months of working together, Melanie is now a proud owner of her own home.

A year-and-a-half later, Melanie has now progressed from being a sole trader to becoming a director of her company, Speaking Styles Pty Ltd.

What you will notice is what Melanie was sharing with me is exactly what most entrepreneurs want - this is a common theme.

We get excited about starting our businesses and very quickly realise that we come in each day putting out fires, focussing on so many things and never seem to focus on our numbers.

I have helped businesses in various niches and enjoy working with service-based business owners and coaches.

In the words of another very dear client of mine:

"Najma might say something different, but I believe it's more about a connection for her. It's not just about the business. It's about people that connect with her and what her values are. At that meeting, she went through how she could help me, and she immediately put me at ease that everything can be achievable."

Neve Cussen, Apple Leaf Interiors

Before working with me, Neve approached bookkeeping the way most business owners do – not thinking about it until tax time, and she would feel a great deal of stress and panic. That stress and family responsibilities made her realise she needed a different approach to managing her money and business finances.

Neve recounts:

"The stress levels were really getting to me. On a personal level, I have two children, and I needed the bookkeeping taken out of my every day. I shouldn't have been coming to that level of stress. With Najma, there's peace of mind and guidance. I call her my fairy because she's always telling me not to stress."

Neve had come to me also wanting to know exactly what was really "happening" in her business. Those closest to her told her she should give up her "hobby".

Like Melanie, she was confused and unsure if her business was making any money. There was no clear direction of what was happening, and she was always hesitant to pay herself.

That peace of mind was critical for Neve, who always says she's quite extroverted and tends to panic, so she feels my kindness and calm personality have helped her feel more at ease. The guidance and consultations provided have helped Neve best allocate her money to reduce her tax obligations and have been invaluable to her.

After going through her numbers and finances, she was able to realise the potential of her business and today, just like Melanie, Neve is now the director of her own company. From hobby to owning a company, I am so proud of what Neve has achieved.

Not knowing how to focus on your numbers or, in fact, anything related to money is not your fault. We were never given a handbook, let alone taught this skill at school. The topic of money is usually a taboo subject. No one wants to talk about money, and it is human nature to avoid the topic. I'm here to tell you it's not your fault, but the worst thing you can do is to avoid asking for help. This is what I am here for: to teach, guide and show you that there is an easier way you can get great results. To witness the joy when I get to tell my clients that their profits earned are not to be reinvested in the business but it's to reward themselves for running their business so well.

Our numbers are the language of our business; let's learn all about it together!

So, to sum up, when people ask me what I do, I say, "I build wells."

Wells?

Wait, aren't I a bookkeeper?

I am, but being a Profit First Professional means I have the power to make my money work for me, with some spare to share around. And I choose to share my profits with those who need safe, reliable water supplies.

I consider myself as just one woman, but the 30 wells and still counting have contributed to over 12,000 water wells for more than 2 million people through Human Appeal. When you work with me as your Profit First Professional, you can also use your profits to build wells or make a difference not just in your life but for others too!

Because you'll have the freedom and power to do any or all of those things once you have clear financial goals and clarity around your money.

It only takes a few months to get from cash flow calamity to money mastery, and all you must do is become intentional and clear about your money.

Business ownership comes with a whole mess of bills and investments and debts and taxes intertwined with your personal finances, so it's important to pick it all apart and ensure you're securely set up both professionally and personally for all that life throws at you.

My own background is in finance, of course, but I've also got plenty of real-life experience juggling family commitments and work.

I would love for you to share your thoughts in my 'Rocket to Profit' private Facebook community group:

www.facebook.com/groups/rockettoprofitcommunity

Like you, business ownership is what I want to do. I want to do it well and want the same for you. I refuse to replicate my parents' overcommitted work lives.

And I want to build a future where no child has to walk an unsafe journey just to find something that should be a basic human right. Because we all deserve better, don't you think?

About the Author

Najma Khan is the owner of La Trobe Bookkeeping and specialises in helping business owners get clarity around their money and finances. Born in South Africa, now residing in sunny Perth, Australia. She is a Certified Mastery Level Profit First Professional and money coach. Najma has empowered, inspired, and guided many business owners to go from struggling with cash flow to clarity & freedom with money in as little as a few months. Najma has been interviewed on many podcasts, such as Flying Solo and Bounce Out of Bed and has been interviewed on business shows. Najma is passionate about her health, people and the belief that one person can change the world. She is on a mission to change how people think about money and to help them realise that "PROFIT" is not a dirty word.

Email: najma@latrobebookkeeping.com.au
Facebook: www.facebook.com/najma.khan.71
Website: https://latrobebookkeeping.com.au/

Natalie Lewis

Mi'djam
(Woman)

"There is nothing concealed that will not be disclosed or hidden that will not be made known.
What you have said in the dark will be heard in the daylight, and what you have whispered in the ear in the inner rooms will be proclaimed from the roofs."

~ Luke 12:2-3

I DID NOT CONSENT

For You to Crush my Thoughts and Mind
So that I would Second Guess Myself,
In the way, You have Treated me

I DID NOT CONSENT

For you to Fore Fill YOUR Twisted Fantasy, to Do
Whatever you wanted and Bruise and Break MY Body.

I DID NOT CONSENT

To Be Disrespected
Treated Less than What You've Hated within Yourself.
In Conversations You may have had.
Convincing Yourself That I was Mad…
You Didn't Want to See the Damage it will Cause
Knowing You'll Get your way, Because of Their Laws
For Silent Eyes and Blinded ears
Our Children are Sitting and Crying in Fear

THEY DID NOT CONSENT

To be Steered Down this Path,
Festering, Lustful, Torment and Scars…

THEY DID NOT CONSENT

Keeping Dark Secrets,
Raping Bodies, Minds and Spirits,

Victims SHOUT, a Disturbing Uproar
IT'S TRUTH-TELLING TIME
THE AWAKENING of LORE

Here I am, standing in my bathroom in front of the mirror naked. I am in shock. My body is hurting inside and out. I can see bruises of big handprints on my breasts and arms.

I'm trying to think about what happened, and the drive home that morning was blurry; I had to keep checking in with myself. I don't remember drinking that much; I took a sip on my second vodka, so what happened?

My pelvic bone and hips painfully throbbing. I couldn't walk; I had to shuffle into the shower.

As the hot water hits my back, and I feel the warmth trickling over my shoulders down my breasts, I can hear a gut-wrenching sobbing. It's me!

BANG! What the Fuck was That?? I was hit with a flash of his face; then, a subtle confusing feeling overcame me. So, I move, grab my towel and shuffle to my closet to dress. I eventually grab my phone and call my oldest and dearest Friend, my sister.

In our conversation, it's dawning on me I am a Victim of Rape.

My heart was sinking, not only for me but for my son. How am I going to tell him?

Because my boy and I have spent years of healing coming through this trauma before. He was a victim of domestic violence and incestual rape.

Now here he is, holding me tight as I break down in his arms; all I can remember is the stony glaze in his eyes.

He was in shock; we all were because the man who did this was supposed to be a respected leader and role model within the

Aboriginal community.

I had to be brave and report it, a matter of practising what I preach. For my boy, for other VICTIMS that COULD NOT speak out, MOST of all for ME.

> Child, it's time to break the shell, Life's gonna hurt, but it's meant to be felt; you cannot touch the sky from inside yourself; you cannot fly until you break the shell.
> ~ India Arie – Break the Shell

These days we see and read more in-your-face honesty and truth-telling coming from our youth. Thanks to social media platforms, such as YouTube, Facebook, Instagram, Tic Tok, Tweets etc., it seems to give people the courage to express whatever is fermenting within themselves.

Whether we agree with the content or not, it's their truth-telling. Although what I have found when it comes to specific topics, especially sexual abuse, rape or incestual rape, it's still a taboo that we dare not speak about.

Seven years of my boys and I healing journey. Being the mother of both perpetrator and victim, I found myself carrying all the guilt, grief, shame and hurt that DID tear my family apart. Little did I know this particular situation was preparing me for my own heart-wrenching experience a few years later. So, here I am, nearing 50 years of age, to humbly impart some of my knowledge from these life-changing experiences. Maybe my story is heard and able to help someone else.

> **At the end of the day, it's not about what you have or even what you've accomplished. It's about what you've done with those accomplishments. It's about who you've lifted up, who you've made better. It's about what you've given back."**
> ~ Denzel H Washington Jnr

This chapter is only a blink in time but had an important impact that was to change everything for whom I am to the Woman I am to become.

I want to leave you feeling empowered and for you to know you are not alone. So, this is me holding my hand out for you to grab onto, let's walk together, All Sisters and Brothers, to be Lifted and Lightened!

Sharing your story and speaking out about what is happening to you mentally, emotionally and physically is a great start to making it through to the next steps.

What are the next steps?

It's not only **Surviving** but also **Conquering**; IT'S **LIVING!**

It doesn't mean that the trauma and negative traumas are to be buried. From my experience, that doesn't work because out of nowhere, something can happen and then we're finding myself triggered back to where we started; it's not sustainable.

The consequences of my actions would be finding myself unable to give any love and attention to anyone, not even myself. A loop that I chose not to leave because I wanted to hold on to the hurt, to be tormented because I couldn't feel anything, I chose anger.

To be honest with you, I was suicidal. From my perspective, there was no other way out. Not even my children could save me. But somewhere subtly inside, it scared me. Because I also lived my life by faith. I truly believe that every single one of us on this earth has a specific part to play, a purpose within our lifetime. Deep down, I knew mine hadn't been fulfilled.

So, I decided to fight. Fight for me. Fight for the unknown that I hadn't experienced yet.

Fight to Live.

We have a choice to say NO! We will not let that person or people in that situation have control and violate us anymore. It stops when you are ready to claim back your mind, claim back your body and let your Spirit sour.

I want to give you a little gift. I will share with you something that helps me in those moments where you feel that peace isn't as present as you would like it to be. When you're going through the processes of reporting the rape and navigating what victims have to go through. The possibility of losing family and friends and being shunned by the community can be overwhelming. Or it could be just the day-to-day emotions, up and downs, feelings of anxiety, and you don't know why?

So, find a place that's comfortable for you to sit or lie down.

You can do this while you're reading or after having a safe space to relax. Then you can close your eyes. Either way, you will feel the benefits from this.

First, Breath in and out nice and steady. With your thoughts, check your body out. Where is the tension? What parts are hurting?

Then when you are ready, I want you to take deep breaths in and out.

Take nice slow breaths all the way to your stomach.

Every time you breathe in, I want you to imagine a glittering show of light floating around you. Within each glitter is a golden healing light.

When you breathe out, I want you to blow all the air out until you have no more.

Visualise that the air you breathe out is black soot, all the emotions that don't serve you for your greatest good. Blow it out.

You can feel all the parts in your body that are tense or hurting and visualise that dark cloudy matter surrounding those areas.

You are seeing it leave your body through every breath you exhale.

You will replace it when you breathe in with the golden glitter of healing light.

Visualise that your body is reacting to this. It's feeling lighter, the pain has lessened, or there is no pain at all.

Now I want you to imagine you're sitting there with yourself. Your higher self is divine and brings with it feelings of angelic harmony and peace.

This is who you truly are, and you are greater and more powerful than what you think.

You are Love and Loved.

Imagine golden rays glowing from every pore of your body.

You can manifest anything in your new life because you are a creator.

You can and will fore fill your purpose.

Sit with that, and keep breathing nice and steady.

IN and OUT.

We are going to keep this Peaceful feeling with us.

When you are ready, I want you to take notice of your breathing.

Slowly listen to the noise around you.

Gently wiggle your fingers and toes.

Start feeling your legs and arms.

Take nice smooth breaths in and out.

Notice how your chest is rising and falling.

Feel your head and mind is clear of tension.

Your body tingles, and you are full of peaceful energy and calm.

Welcome Back, People, to a peaceful you!

This is something you can do anytime. Amen.

Just like the mythological Arabian bird, the Phoenix. There comes a time when you will rise from the ashes of the woman you were and emerge as a Woman of Strength, Power and Divine Love.

I was blessed with a job that I loved. Working with amazing people and an organisation was continually growing to better the community. I was the first aboriginal person to be in a role like this, and I assisted and resourced the organisation to build relationships and better understand First Nations culture and cultural practices. Walking together towards Reconciliation.

Now, after my rape last year, my whole view of what I was doing as work seemed insignificant compared to this. How can I continue building relationships in the name of Reconciliation when there are dark secrets in our communities that don't represent, Respect, Honour and Truth?

Blackfellas are hurting their own. I couldn't get my head around it. Here we are marching in solidarity for our sovereign rights and sharing common anger and hate for the injustices that our people suffer at the hands of The Crown, Government and Law enforcement. First Nations People who are presenting themselves to the wider communities and society as leaders, role models, Directors, and Chair of Boards of First Nations Organisations. Cultural Leaders are marching thousands of our people in the name of Sovereignty, and yet what happens behind the veil of deceit is nothing to do with culture. It's pure evil. Because keeping the secrets is allowing this to continue.

In my experience with the whole process as a victim, it is evident that there are gaps within all services that were set up to provide support. Trauma after trauma, from the hospital, the police, and victims assist with counselling for domestic violence and sexual assault. How I was treated as a victim, as a woman, as an Aboriginal Woman. I couldn't believe what I had to endure. But I went through it all. I didn't give up even though I wanted to most of the time. I made myself go through everything because if I was finding it hard, I can't imagine what it is like for my people in the community who struggle through life worse than me.

My Spirit needed healing, so I went back to the country.

My country is Juru, part of the Birra Gubba Nation. It is located in the Burdekin District, North Queensland. A little town called Ayr.

So, when I returned home, I decided I would make it my business to change things for the better for victims of rape and incestual rape within our communities.

I wanted to first resource who and what we had in place for First Nations Women for healing. Then I found a connection.

Sharon Malone is a Wakka Wakka woman born in Cherbourg. Who had her own battles of incestual rape. Sharon, like myself, believes that it is up to our generation to show up, speak out and make a safer community and place to talk about these issues for the next generation. Our purpose of why we will be working together was becoming clearer. She like the "Ya'djin Yudoo Wung-Gu" women group based in Brisbane are going to Speak Out and Loud for the Rights of All Victims.

What would it take to keep our own people accountable for the violence they inflict on our own communities over and over again?

Would this open up the possibility for conversations regarding when the western law fails our people, we then turn to our cultural practices of Lore?

We are Women! We are Creators of our own Queendom.

It starts with one courageous person at a time, just like the women in "Breaking SILENT Codes", a video clip you can watch on YouTube where First Nation Women from All nations come together in New York 2020. If you want to know more about the movement or want to support our Amazing Courageous First Nations Sisters, please don't hesitate to contact me.

> It is YABU who arms me with STRENGTH & keeps my way secure.
> ~ 2 Samuel 22:33

About the Author

Natalie Lewis is a Juru Woman (Aboriginal) and of South Sea Islander Descent. Natalie is part of the 'Stolen Generation' from the early 1970s. Her story has been featured on 'Jigs Saw' podcast, an Australian Adoption Agency on Spotify and Uniting Care QLD's internal Cultural Awareness Training.

She has worked for the Uniting Aboriginal & Islander Christian Congress for the last ten years. 2019 Natalie was a First Nations Resourcing Officer, working for the Uniting Church Australia Queensland Synod. Being the first Aboriginal Person in that position in Queensland.

Natalie has created a movement called 'I Did Not Consent', working and supporting First Nations Women's Groups and young peoples of rape and incestual rape within their communities. Natalie spends her time off relaxing by baking cakes, playing with her puppy and loving on the adult and young children she adopts within the community.

Facebook: www.facebook.com/Natalie Lewis
Email: ididnotconsent22@gmail.com

Voices of Impact

Alissa Meechan

"If you could be exactly who you are, who would you be?"
~ Alissa Meechan Self-Mastery Initiator

December 2016 saw me sitting in the passenger's seat of our car. Hubby and I were on our way to visit family in our hometown. It was a beautiful day for a road trip. A great day to be alive, and here I was … empty, hollow, stuck, lost … downright miserable! And absolutely terrified that I would never feel happy again.

You see, I'd found myself in a place I recognised. This wasn't a physical place; it was a mental and emotional place. I recognised it because I'd been here before, back in 2010. But back then, it had been worse—deeper and darker. It scared me to know that even though I wasn't as deeply absorbed in it as I had been, I knew that I was well on my way.

2010 saw me at 39 years of age, married, with two teenage children, a business partner in a business with a seven-figure income and a carer to my father. Saying it like that makes it sound easy like it could fit into a box with a neat little bow on top. But this was not the reality I felt I was living.

At the time, I did not feel supported by my husband at home or in the business. The relationship between my business partner and I was strained. Did I mention my kids were teenagers? Why is there no manual for teenagers! And, in amongst all of that, Dad's cancer had reappeared, and he now needed chemo. Consequently, I needed to work out a way to fit in, taking my dad to the hospital each week for 6 weeks for his treatments. I felt stretched to the limit; however, I needed to stretch more.

I was advised Dad's treatment would be quick with possible side effects of mild flu-like symptoms. In reality, it took 13 weeks to get through the treatments; multiple doctor's appointments, prescriptions, pathology and occasional ambulance call-outs, which ended up with hospitalisation for approximately 4 weeks. And still not the end of it! Within about a week of being out of the hospital, Dad's health started to decline again. He refused to go back to the hospital in the ambulance and was too sick to get to the doctor. It was stressful for everyone in the family, and realistically we were all struggling.

When taking any time off work, I would receive numerous phone calls from my business partner to attend to business matters which were impossible to do from home. In desperation, I went to see our doctor's surgery and refused to leave until they said they would get a doctor out to do a home visit. The doctor, who eventually attended, had been advised of Dad's health issues and was therefore aware that, in my opinion, Dad was suicidal. I can still vividly recall Dad telling the doctor that had he been able to get to his medication; her visit would have been unnecessary. Nothing can prepare you for hearing those words!

I didn't realise it at the time, but this doctor was my hero. As she went to leave our house, she asked me to visit the surgery the next day at 9 am. I remember feeling concerned that there was something else wrong with Dad; however, what she said to me shook me to my core. She advised me my dad was going to be fine, that we had done a fantastic job of looking after him, and she was more concerned about me. I was the one that needed help, and she was going to do exactly that.

The next day, I left her office with a script for medication, a referral for a psychologist and ongoing appointments with her to check in on my progress. My health and life were improving.

So why did I find myself back in that space again in 2016?

Because while the medication and psychologist allowed me to control my depression, stress, overwhelm and anxiety, it didn't get rid of them. For me, the medication was a band-aid solution. It allowed me to believe I was in control, but I hadn't dealt with the issues behind the emotions, which meant when I went off the medication, even though I had some tools from the psychologist, for me, they weren't enough for ongoing success.

Keeping control for me was a bit like my efforts in gardening. Now, I'm not a very good gardener, but something I can do is grow weeds. With some weeds, you can treat the plant once, and it will never bother you again. However, at other times the best we can see happening is that we can control the weed. We trim it back and try our best to restrict it from taking over an area. And all goes smoothly ... until it doesn't. Until, for some reason, we turn our backs and forget what we were doing. We get distracted. Then we turn around and what was a nice neat little controlled weed is suddenly huge, out of control, and no matter what we try, it doesn't seem to bring it back to a controllable level.

This is my way of explaining how my unconscious overthinking led to my emotions getting out of control. With the help of medication and regular psychologist appointments, I had been able to make a conscious effort to keep my thoughts and emotions in control. I kept focusing on what was important and, for the most part, felt in control of my life. As life became busier, I lost that learned ability to focus on what I needed and allowed my fear of letting others down to take over. I started making decisions based in guilt and fear, and then I'd feel like a failure if the outcome was less than perfect. This led to a downward spiral of more decisions based in guilt or fear.

With each significant relationship, I had given myself a label of who I was to them: wife, mother, daughter, employer, employee, business partner, and carer. With each label, I wore a different mask, and with each mask, there were certain expectations and responsibilities that came with them. What I didn't notice was that the person I was, was not always seen by others. The labels I had put on myself to make it easier for me to determine who I was, were mixed together, layered and confused. I had no idea where one ended, and another started. I was out of control, and so was the world I lived in.

This is the place I recognised in 2016. And with that recognition came a fear with the realisation that if I didn't find someone to help me get rid of this pattern, I would continue down this path.

However, my biggest fear was not that this would be my life pattern; it was that this pattern would continue to spiral out of control until I chose to stop it. To stop me.

I had seen the repercussions of what suicide could do to a family as I had witnessed it first-hand in 2005 when my brother took his life. It's only been recently that I could admit to myself that I was bordering as close as I was. But even then, with my view dimmed as it was in 2016, I knew that I was uncomfortably close.

This was my turning point. The pivotal moment that I decided to change things. With that, I made a call to a woman I'd known casually for 20 years. I had a 1-hour conversation with her, which led to 5 intensive hours of work over two sessions, and 6 months later, I could honestly say that I was no longer affected by depression, anxiety, stress, and overwhelm. My overall mood had lifted, my head was clearer, and I was enjoying my family, friends and life in general.

I learnt so much about myself and the world I was living in within those 5 short hours that the changes in me started instantly and are still continuing today. I learnt that the choices I had been making, the ones based around guilt and fear of letting people down, were doing exactly that. I had been setting myself up for failure by focusing on what I did not want. And by trying to be everything to everyone, I had lost sight of who I truly was. Everyone was being let down. Everyone including me

The challenge I faced moving through this was choosing me.

Choosing a path for me and a place for me in my world. Not necessarily apart from anyone else but including them while ensuring that I came first. Not in the generally perceived, selfish way. But in a way, that meant I was ready to grow and nurture myself. And then, after I did this, I would be able to nurture and grow others and help them and be of service to them.

The modality that I was initially introduced to was Time Line Therapy. I was so inspired by the results I achieved and found it so life-changing that I chose to study this modality. In August 2017, I completed the practitioner's training and then went on to do the Master Practitioners' training in December 2017.

Along with my certification in Time Line Therapy, I also received certification in Neurolinguistic Programming and Hypnotherapy. I was eager to learn more and so the energy modalities of Forensic Healing, Energy and Soul Medicine and Reiki followed. In 2019, I trained to become a qualified coach and speaker ... bringing all these learned modalities together under one banner. Therefore, I could customise my coaching packages, ensuring that clients' specific needs were met and not a one size fits all approach.

Throughout my journey, I have discovered there are so many accessible resources and nine times out of ten, we are unaware of their existence and availability to us. There are many people enhancing their own lives by combining their learnings of life and chosen modalities with a willingness to teach others their successful processes, and that's where I find myself today. I'm still learning about myself, and I'm still bringing that forward, but I'm also taking that into the public as well and teaching other people.

Being the Self-Mastery Initiator means that my guidance has clients implementing and regulating their own self-mastery. It's wonderful to see the growth in my clients; The self-assurance that they gain; The calmness in their control of themselves. I have many clients which have come to me with those labels of anxiety, overwhelm, depression and stress and have now learnt to control those emotions. Not in a way that they are overcontrolling them and not feeling any emotions. They are still feeling emotions; however, they now know that any negative emotions they feel will pass. The previous highs and lows that once resembled a crazy rollercoaster ride have now levelled out.

Once, when I asked a client how she was going, she mentioned how much her emotions had settled for her. Her highs were just as high, if not higher. Her lows, however, hadn't been happening. She wasn't losing her temper or lashing out in anger. This surprised and confused her, and she was genuinely concerned when she asked if this was a *normal* outcome. It was so far out of her normal that, even though she had envisioned being like this, it felt a bit uncomfortable to start with. It took less than 24 hours for her to be totally comfortable and send me a message laughing at herself for having asked such a question.

Another client who was referred to me had been admitted to the hospital with a suspected heart attack that was eventually diagnosed as a severe panic attack. She had a high-stress job, was newly married with a blended family and had moved into a new house which was also being renovated. Anger and sadness were a regular part of her day—if not bursting forth, then bubbling under the surface. Her dilemma was based on her need to control each and every situation while not being perceived as controlling. She was, in her words, a self-confessed 'Control Freak'. The more in control she tried to be, the less in control she felt.

After her second session, she already 'didn't recognise herself', as the change was so huge. Even her family and friends had noticed her changes. She was calmer, more relaxed, and happier. Her newly re-found direction and clarity meant that her to-do list was being ticked off each day, and she was finding she had spare time on her hands to do the things she previously didn't have time for.

An unexpected bonus was that she had overcome her fear of heights. This was not an issue that she had mentioned in any of our sessions previously. She had been away on holiday, and someone she was with asked if she was doing ok. She had no idea what they were talking about until they explained that they were on a platform that previously would have had her overwhelmed in fear. The fear was gone completely. She found the skills she learnt amazing and continues to use them today.

In order to work with me, clients are initially informed of what obligations they will need to meet in order to achieve their proposed outcomes.

1. They need to be open in both their responses to me and in

regard to the things I ask them to consider. They need to be fully honest and be willing to play full out. By this, I mean that they are willing to do whatever it takes to have their problems disappear.

2. Be accountable for the decisions they have made in the past and are making in the now. This means understanding that sometimes the decisions they make—including the decisions they decide not to make—do not always end in the ways predicted. Choosing to learn from these decisions is every bit as important as celebrating the wins. No more finding excuses and playing the blame game.

Their lives are where they are because of the choices they have made in the past. Being consciously aware of those choices means that they have the power to act on what needs to be changed as it is needed. The ball is in their court.

I fully understand making changes can be scary, and there are times when they will want to resist those changes; however, acceptance and action are key to achieving their desired results. No one else can do this for them, but I am here to ease them into this transition.

3. To be conscious of what they are projecting. Preconceived ideas dictate our thoughts, feelings and emotions. The more positive they are in their perceptions, the more positive their projections will be. Focussing continually on what is not wanted, liked or needed will consequently attract more negative thoughts and experiences to them, both consciously and

unconsciously. Teaching my clients to be conscious of what they are thinking and saying is one of the biggest skills I believe I will teach them.

Of course, there are things that they are going to require from themselves to be able to make the changes too. Firstly, they will need to get rid of their negative emotions, beliefs and decisions that are impacting their lives. This is the area that I help them with initially with Time Line Therapy and then with the follow-up coaching.

Next, they need to take the action they have committed to. They will be required to do what needs to be done to achieve the outcome they are seeking. This requires them to be accountable for their actions and to enforce boundaries—theirs and the people around them.

Lastly, they need to focus on what they want. So often, I will hear my clients tell me what they don't like or don't want to happen. When I ask what they do want, they are at a loss. They are unsure as they have never given it any thought. Something I help them with is to get clarity around their desired outcome by asking them what it is and then what they think they will see, hear, feel and know about themselves when they have achieved it, allowing them to form a detailed image and goal to move towards.

Currently, there is so much dialogue around topics of healing our past hurts—inner child, generational, past life—and while they may have played a significant part in how you were raised, if they are blocking you from moving forward into a future you want, then you need to make a choice to do something about it. You are the oldest and wisest you have ever been. You have more experience and wisdom about your own values and beliefs than you did when all of those hurts occurred. Choose to use that experience and wisdom to be the best you can be.

The ability to master your thoughts, emotions and beliefs allows you to become the master of yourself. Mastering yourself means that the outside world, while it affects you, does not control you. It means that you can understand that although not everyone sees the world the way you do, you are able to respect them and their view anyway.

My ultimate goal is to educate people globally. How? Through self-acceptance, self-love and self-empowerment, you can respect everyone's opinion and love them, even if their point of view is not right for you. Life is less about being right or wrong and more about understanding where others are coming from.

About the Author

Alissa Meechan was raised in a small coal-mining town in North Queensland, Australia. She now lives on an acreage outside of Mackay with her husband, enjoying the peace and quiet of the area. Now aged 51, it took her 44 years and a near-total mental and emotional breakdown to work out what she wanted to be when she grew up.

Known as the Self-Mastery Initiator, Alissa believes that a world of unconditional acceptance and love starts with being able to appreciate and express your own uniqueness. Her passion is coaching her clients to be their best versions of themselves.

Alissa states, "I believe we make life more difficult for ourselves than it needs to be. We accept and give ourselves labels so that we and others feel comfortable. But these labels may define us wrongly and limit our true potential. And who truly wants that?"

Website: www.alissameechan.com
Email: hello@alissameechan.com
Facebook: www.facebook.com/AlissaMeechanSelfMastery

Kären Moroney

"I did not create a dream, I did not borrow a dream, I was given a dream" Sarah Henderson" Strength to Strength, An Autobiography'; Sarah Henderson; Thomas Dunne Books, March 2000

Oh, the icy air, cold, so very, very cold. Instinctively I wrap my coat around me just that bit tighter. I should have realised; I should have known the cold here in this far-flung Northern country, all wrapped up in its white finery, innocent in its beauty, yet ferocious in its bone-numbing sting. It's minus 30^c outside; the air is crisp and cold as I leave the warmth of Gardermoen, Norway's International Airport. I take out a piece of paper containing the instructions to find my way to Hamar. Making my way to the train station, I understand none of the signage; it's all in Norwegian. I feel nervous yet excited to be back. The last time I was here, it was early Autumn; the air was balmy but still carrying the signature notes of chill. My husband Wayne and I had travelled here on our first big European adventure. Part of the time, we travelled with my father and mother. Instinctively I felt myself smiling; it had been a great holiday, ten weeks of travelling the length and breadth of the UK, Scandinavia and as far south as Italy. We had hired a car in London and driven it all over Europe, at a time when tourists took Contiki Tours rather than hire cars.

This time I am alone; it is a business trip. It's 1994, and Norway or more specifically, Lillehammer, is firmly in the media spotlight. Norway is hosting the Winter Olympic Games.

There are signs everywhere hailing this international event. There is an expectation in the air and lots of bustle around me as people enter the train and claim their seats. I sit down, glad to feel the warmth of the train carriage wrap around me. Instinctively I cradle my emerging belly; I am five months pregnant. Checking the time, I wind my watch back nine hours. I make sure my ticket is close at hand and finally lean back and close my eyes. I think of my two sons at home with their father and harbour a sense of guilt. Do good mothers take off to the other side of the earth to fulfil a business invitation? After all, it's not like a party invitation, where we can tuck our babies into their beds, give last-minute instructions to the babysitter and know we will be back before they wake in the morning. I reassure myself I did the right thing in hiring a nanny for the two weeks I will be away. Wayne will be busy on our dairy farm, and the boys will be well cared for. Pushing these thoughts to the back of my mind, I concentrate on what has brought me to this place.

***

It was the end of winter, August 28, 1989; nothing remarkable about that, but in fact, it was. That day, that winter's end heralded the beginning of a momentous change in my life. I was 28 years old.

It was the day we buried my father.

Literally overnight, I found myself jettisoned into unfamiliar roles. The director and agent of a genetic trade import company, director of two live cattle import syndicates, editor and publisher of the International Red Cow magazine, executive officer of an emerging international red cow organisation and a new partner in the family dairy farm enterprise

I had inherited a fledgling genetics business that neither I nor anyone else in my family knew anything about!

I embraced this foreign space. My father had given me a dream, and I decided to nurture it, rise to the challenge and embark on the adventure. The weight of expectations from business clients and the support of family was integral to galvanising me into action.

The responsibilities and pressure on me were inordinate. Wayne and I had already made an enormous lifestyle change only months earlier. We had left our city jobs; I had given birth to our first son Kane who was five weeks old, and we had sold our house and moved back to the family farm. Renovations to the original homestead had progressed slowly, so we had to live with my mother and grandmother for the first eight months. Being a person who likes structure and organisation, this felt like utter chaos!

I grappled with the weight of coping with all these changes while grieving the loss of my father. The next twelve months were like a baptism of fire, creating an awakening in me.

I took files to bed at night, and in between night feeds with my new baby, I began to learn the business. While my baby digested his milk, I digested business contracts and the state of our finances. I discovered that my father, true to form, was not into any small business; this 'thing' had tentacles around the globe; I was both aghast and brimming with pride.

During the day, between being a wife and mother, farm business partner and businesswoman, I answered faxes and made phone calls around the globe, reassuring business clients that I was at the helm of the genetics business now, and it was business as usual. The fact was, I had no real idea what I was doing. I worked hard to reassure clients and worried about the details later.

My previous work experience had set me in good stead to handle the administration, promotion and media sides of the business. I had worked as a bookkeeper and later in commercial radio. This part of my working life was during the 80's - a decade synonymous with 'Big': big hairdos, big shoulder pads, big business. We witnessed big deals, big corporate collapses, big tax evasion and the big share market crash, followed shortly by big economic reform and big, painful adjustments. However, Australia emerged on the other side with economic reforms that have made us strong today. Maybe the analogy is somewhat disproportionate, but I felt I was going through a similar life cycle. Everything consisted of big challenges and steep learning curves. It was both exciting and full of uncertainty and risks. Nevertheless, I was determined to give this business my best shot!

Nestled in the rich and picturesque Mitta Valley in Northeast Victoria, my upbringing on our generational-owned dairy farm was a happy one. I loved the outdoor life and learned from an early age how to milk cows, change irrigation rotations, muster and work cattle, ride horses and to handle the farm vehicles. Looking back, we were given lots of responsibility at a young age, and I can't help feeling it was the training ground for much of what unfolded in my later years.

My father's mantra was he was not going to raise 'useless kids', so the work ethic was instilled in us at an early age. I had three siblings, one older sister and two younger brothers. There were no 'sleep ins', and everyone had jobs to complete either before or after school.

My father was the dominant force in our family life. Coming from a Scottish / Irish pedigree, he embodied the best and worst of the traits often associated with the kin of this heritage.

Big and brisk, his voice I remember with clarity. Deep and resonating, it always commanded the attention of a room and of course, he was the centrepiece of our family. I both feared and adored him. Intelligent, quick of wit and with the ability to think outside the box, he could just as easily soothe with a word and then cut you with another.

My mother, on the other hand, was stoic, hard-working, practical, and compliant. Her early years were not easy, having fled her home country of Estonia during the war years. Her family arrived in Australia under the 'Displaced Persons' migration policy of the day, arriving in 1949 to Bonegilla Migration Camp Albury, NSW. With virtually the clothes on their backs, speaking limited English, and a few wooden trunks to their name, their life had to begin all over again. I recall, with humour, Mother saying, "It was quite a shock our arrival in Bonegilla; our father had told us we were going to a place where the weather is always warm, there is no snow and that bananas are growing everywhere." In fact, they arrived in Bonegilla in mid-Winter, in a blanket of fog, and there was not a banana in sight!

***

I became an Adventurer in those early years after my father's passing. I worked hard to stabilise the genetics business here in Australia and with our overseas suppliers. I identified the priorities and layers in the business while building my personal profile based on reliability, good communication and trust. Among the tools I utilised was the publication my father had established called 'The Red Cow International', a magazine supported by the red and red and white coated dairy breeds of the world. It was a unique magazine, ambitious in its scope and content. Using the networks I had re-established after my father's passing, I sourced articles and advertising from farmers, scientists, and genetic companies around the globe. Publishing twice a year, the magazine was an ever-present occupation and afforded me an amazing platform to build my professional profile. The following years saw me frequently travelling to the

Scandinavian countries of Sweden, Norway and Denmark, where our main suppliers of dairy genetics were sourced. Here I would tour the breeder barns and AI centres. I viewed potential new bulls and their progeny for import into the Australian market while writing articles about the farmers we were sourcing the genetics from. I soon learnt that people love to share their stories and showcase their operations. Working in tandem with the magazine was the International Red Dairy Breeds Federation (IRDBF), which I proudly led. The prime purpose of this organisation was to bring the red-coated dairy breeders of the world together on a regular basis. A global exchange of knowledge and information centred around a conference and tours of farms and farming systems by the host country. I was the Executive Officer of this organisation for over 20 years, and in that period, I was privileged to help organise and facilitate these inspirational events from South Africa to Sweden, Norway, the USA, Germany and, of course, Australia.

Like an Adventurer that focuses on conquering one level at a time, I had developed the framework, built important networks and shaped the business model to reinforce and grow the Aussie red dairy cow business.

By now, I had three beautiful sons at varying stages of maturity. With my youngest son Blake now 15 years old, I felt they were independent enough for me to continue the adventure and take the business to the next level.

Some eight years previous, Wayne and I also purchased my mother and my brother's shares in the dairy farm, giving us sole ownership. Anyone who is involved in agriculture knows it's a volatile industry to work in. We are subject to many external pressures and often ones we can't control, be that commodity prices, interest rates or the weather. I have experienced them all, navigating through a decade-long drought, the Global Financial Crisis, floods and, more recently, the infamous 'milk price clawbacks'. All playing havoc with our bottom line and long-term sustainability.

This volatility fuelled my desire to take the genetics business to the next level creating a diversification of income.

From an agency, the business evolved to become the sole importers, marketers, and distributors of the products, therefore giving me control from product entry to exit. I was supported by my overseas suppliers and the next two years saw the business go from strength to strength. Each year saw an upwards curve, achieving sales exceeding any number of units sold since the first importation of semen into Australia, 21 years previous. I had really made the dream a reality and was leading from a position of strong self-belief, internal intuition and courage. I was, however, not prepared for what lay ahead.

By the third year, I started to encounter difficulties with the business. The reality is those successful start-up companies like mine become targets for manoeuvres and takeovers. After long and protracted negotiations with those involved, I decided that our values and principles were mismatched, and we separated ways. My biggest disappointment in all that transpired was that the people I had valued, trusted, and loved had betrayed me.

At this point, I want to stress that developing leadership skills is so important in surviving and thriving in any business environment. Why? Because, like my experience, unexpected things happen to throw us off course.

Betrayal, in my case, became a catalyst for reform. It galvanised my determination and re-energised the self-starter within me.

I chose to lead by making decisions that were right for the business and my family and then moved forward with purpose. Today I continue to run a genetics company named 'Auzred XB'. The experience taught me valuable lessons, and I found the courage to rebuild and expand my expertise in the business. I took on a business partner with complementary skills. We identified a niche market and refocused our efforts on three-way crossbreeding, working with one of the leading professors in this area of research and breeding. Together, we share the risks and responsibilities, a freedom I had previously not experienced. I can honestly say that there is no such thing as failure – only feedback. It's critical to persist until we discover the right way to get things to work. With the right attitude and genuine commitment, success will follow!

Regarding our farming enterprise, we now have the fifth generation ready to take over the reins. We are in the transition phase; as Wayne and I prepare to take a step back in the business, it's time to change gears to allow for new adventures.

For the last ten years, I have pledged some of my time to serve as a director on various industry boards and community organisations, my accumulated experience, skills and knowledge, have been instrumental in serving in this capacity. I have also been fortunate to have found a mentor who has selflessly, over the last ten years, shared her corporate and personal experiences with me. Although Desirée's leadership journey has been through the corporate sector in a diverse range of industries, the challenges, barriers, and issues are uncannily similar. Desirée tells me that she has watched me mature and grow into an authentic leader that can seamlessly transition from the milking shed to the boardroom.

***

I know what has bought me to this place; it is here, right in front of me. From this point, I have the perfect panorama of our farm stretched out before me.

It is late afternoon, and the sun is sinking. The mountains that cradle the long narrow valleys begin to cast their afternoon shadows. Today, the subtle change of shadow and light is gentle and non-intrusive, conveying a sense of calmness. Yet I've witnessed other times when storm clouds gather and wild winds whip up the hills, how threatening and destabilising it can be. A lot like life itself.

I smile. Gazing down the hill and at the edge of my vision, I see the backs of our red cows trailing off towards the dairy for milking. Is it that time already?

As a child, I would peek through the French doors in our home, sitting very quietly so as not to alert my parents to my presence and, with my ear squeezed to the crack, listen to the conversations beyond. Our house was no stranger to people, and the conversations always seemed to revolve around cows. I was intrigued; what could possibly be so interesting that all they ever talked about was cows? Ironically, I find my own life is so fundamentally centred on these same beautiful creatures, and I never tire of talking about them. Many of my best and worst life experiences have been because of a cow.

In the early days, I often felt like a newborn calf; its first entrance into life is not always gentle or easy. It will lay splayed on the ground while its mother will lick and clean the membranes away, allowing it to breathe. Soon the calf is standing, wobbling on its hindlegs and trembling at the knees, half-up and half-down, almost like trying to resolve a dilemma.

The mother will gently nudge her body towards the life source, her precious milk. Soon the calf becomes strong, nurtured by its mother and the efforts of the herd around her. As she matures, she finds her place and voice in the herd and starts to speak out, rising to the challenges and overcoming the obstacles in her path. Finally and unashamedly, she starts to lead with heart and determination. She is another strong and resilient female.

***

At this juncture in my life, I know I have experienced amazing and fortuitous adventures. So many life stories born from this journey, too many to tell here and many more to come.

To my father, I salute you; you trusted me with your dream; not only did I make it a reality, but it created a fire in me to succeed. Although your life was short, I want you to know you played a pivotal role in mine.

Acknowledgements: Wayne, you did not always agree with my choices, but you never tried to block my passage or stop me from being my authentic self; I love you. To my sons, Kane, Mitch and Blake, you are my heart and the best of my life's work. To my nearest confidants, you are empowering human beings; when I am around you, I feel like I can conquer the world; thank you for being there for me.

About the Author

Karen is a fourth-generation dairyfarmer, born and raised in the Mitta Valley, situated in North East Victoria. She is a Director and partner in the dairy operation, 'Arrajarra', and the Co-Owner of Auzred XB, an AI distribution Company focused on three-way crossbreeding and the use of red genetics.

She understands the changing environment and challenges farmers face on a daily basis and has dedicated many years to contributing not only to projects that empower her local community but also to the broader dairy industry by stepping up to lead on Boards and industry groups.

Giving voice to and helping solve issues in an industry she is passionate about has been an important driver for Karen both in business and the farming enterprise. She has a Diploma In HRM and is a Graduate of the Australian Institute of Company Directors.

Email: karen.auzredxb@gmail.com
Facebook: Auzred Xb
Website: www.auzredxb.com.au

Voices of Impact

Susie Moore

"When your clarity meets your conviction, and you apply action to the equation, your world will begin to transform before your eyes."
~ Lisa Nichols – Motivational Speaker
(motivatingthemasses.com)

I come to you as someone who is a work in progress. I have recognised this will be a lifelong discovery. By sharing my story, I hope to help others to take a leap of faith with me and explore the process of clarity seeking. As you read this chapter, I invite you to visualise the creation of your life blueprint. Imagine going into any situation, personal or professional, knowing you have the tools and practices to reveal clarity. The clarity for yourself and others can set you on a path to create the change you seek. Our purpose and sense of clarity can shift as we grow, change, and transform.

- Do you have any areas of your life or work where you have untapped potential?

- Are you a clarity seeker too?

For years, I was stuck in the space of feeling unfulfilled, unsure of my direction, identity, and purpose.

A deep knowing reminded me there were many more sides to

my life, including my career, demanding exploration and work to ensure I could discover my true purpose. Inspired by people with boundless confidence, certainty and intent, I was intrigued by how confidently they led themselves, aligned to purpose and clarity. I knew my purpose was calling me, asking me to reveal it by peeling back the layers of dirt, soil, and clay created by the noise of day-to-day existence.

The turning point was my 27th birthday, and the purpose call volume was turned up to a booming 10, and the panic set in. That muffled voice turned into a loud banging. The ticking of time was getting louder, and my internal narrative went into overdrive:

- "You should know what you want to do with your life by now."
- "Your life will be over when you have kids; you better get cracking."
- "How can you be a mother and guide a child when you don't know who you are?"
- "Have you lived your life and made decisions listening to the wrong voice? What do you really want?"
- "You've lost any connection to spirituality and sense of connectedness."
- "You don't even know your biological dad or sister."

What resulted from this rude awakening was a hectic and determined path of self-discovery. But, first, I had to find a way to clear the layers of dirt, soil, and clay to uncover my true sense of self – to enable progress and answer these enduring questions: a) how could I move forward? b) how am I going to determine the answers? c) how could I be sure this was what I truly wanted?

I started with a bucket list of everything I wanted to achieve. But, I needed more clarity and structure to this plan. So, I turned to a tool I used in my working life as an analyst, mind-mapping. I intended to use these tools to use creative visualisation to shake loose from my fixed mindset, helping reveal the parts of myself waiting to be seen beneath. Writing down my intentions on paper and visualising through mind-maps helped me get specific and purposeful with my goals. The next stage was about me making it happen.

Recalling an experience from my childhood with Buddhist chanting as a small child in Wellington, New Zealand, reinforced the need for me to practice mindfulness to achieve these goals. When I first attended, I was holding my Aunt's hand. As we walked towards the auditorium doors, I could hear a deep rhythmic sound, getting louder and louder. They were chanting Namu myōhō renge kyō (sokaglobal.org), which is Japanese for "devotion to the mystic law of the lotus sutra". I didn't understand it, but it was mesmerising, and I could feel the vibration right through my body. This left an impression as a child about how powerful those words felt, but I had never properly investigated it until my mini-life crisis. The intention of chanting is that it enables us to change our karma and empowers us to steer our fate to our highest potential.

The more I learned, the more I realised that practising mindful concentration could help me in my journey to create the change I was seeking, both internally and externally and ultimately to find the clarity I sought. So I began to chant daily every morning from my bedroom to help set myself up for the day. What did this mean to me? It was manifesting and calling to my best and highest self every day to be present. Through this daily practice, my world would start to shift as the universe heard my call.

Over time, this practice provided many moments of clarity. First, there was work for me to seek opportunities out, take some risks actively, and put myself out there. The reward was rediscovering, learning, and releasing myself from stories that were holding me back. The narrative in my head changed from that negative tone to one of gratitude and the freedom to embrace the moment. With each experience, my self-discovery deepened:

- 2010 Finding my sister after 23 years apart -> "I am grateful to be whole again."
- 2012 Marrying my life partner -> "I am grateful to have someone who loves me unconditionally."
- 2012 Meeting my sister and her family in person -> "I am filled with joy."
- 2015 Training and completing my first Tough Mudder -> "I am strong."
- 2016 Learning to ride motorcycles -> "I am brave."
- 2016 Attending TEDx conference -> "I am curious."
- 2016 Losing my biological dad -> "I am heartbroken."

- 2016 Falling pregnant after four years of trying -> "I am going to be a loving mum."

When I finally became pregnant, I was content with a sense of readiness and anticipation like a racehorse standing behind the starting gates. Having "done the work" and read all the books, surely I was ready for the next chapter of life...right? Well, if you're a parent, I can picture a wry smile appearing on your face right now, as you know that this is what I now understand to be the calm before the storm! Remember when I said, "I come to you as someone who is still growing and improving, and I will continue to be through all my life stages" this was my strongest reminder yet of "the why".

When I held our long-awaited daughter in my hands, she had big brown eyes that pierced straight into my soul, her head was full of short black hair, and she had a beautiful caramel-brown skin tone, courtesy of her dad. Through sleep-deprived eyes, I had an overwhelming feeling of immense gratitude and a genuine appreciation of how precious and fragile life was. Watching her was a miracle; I would wait with bated breath for each smile, coo or cry. We all start out life as sweet little beings, unaware of what it has in store for us. Then, two days in, the wheels began to wobble, my milk had not arrived, and things were getting extremely painful. It got to the third night in the hospital - my daughter was crying because she had the hangers bad. It had just turned midnight, and my husband and I were delirious, listening to my 90's playlist, when the milk let-down finally happened, and she experienced her first milk-induced sleep. Oh, my goodness, this stuff was potent! While she was asleep, we celebrated that win, swinging her white flannel onesies in the air and singing Boney M's Brown Girl in the Ring. We were euphoric.

From that moment on, nothing has come as expected or scheduled, and although it was a steep learning curve, the responsibility I have towards this little person has helped me understand that it's okay. This little pocket rocket would be my personal compass and teacher; she would force me to prioritise what's important and make me realise that my growth and personal work are **never** done.

With this newly found sense of responsibility, I wanted to ensure I gave this beautifully fierce soul the best chance of leading her life as a whole, confident and content person. I know that if I can live life with a clarity of self, purpose and service, I can better model this to my daughter. It also makes me a more understanding and supportive wife, daughter, sister and friend. I can be more empathetic - not only to myself but to others.

When I am faced with situations or decisions where I feel unworthy, I ask questions like, "*Would I allow my daughter to be treated this way?*", "*Would I talk to my daughter this way?*", "*Would I want her to have the courage to take these opportunities?*".
The answers to these questions give me the courage to show up, not just for her but for that little girl still in me that I am now brave enough to encourage.

Have you experienced transitions in life that have changed your perspective?

Having just had my first baby and looking to ease myself back into work, it was a daunting prospect trying to juggle decisions across career and life goals. I was feeling conflicted between ensuring that I had the time and energy to be a good mum while also finding and fulfilling my passion. My ever-supportive husband was my biggest cheerleader, always being that voice of support and drive when mine had quit. However, I looked around and saw many talented people moving up the corporate ladder, one or two rungs at a time, and I just had to take the first step.

I started with a personality test to understand how I interacted in team dynamics, but that didn't give me clarity on how to get closer to my core purpose. So I kept looking and discovered a purpose-driven assessment called Sparketype (sparketype.com/assessment). I loved the structure of the 10 Sparktypes; it helped me reflect and increase my self-awareness. It resonated well with me, noting not everything was 100% accurate, but it helped me identify the gap, those remaining layers of dirt, soil and clay I was struggling to uncover. My primary purpose was being an *Essentialist*, which is the drive to distil, organise and simplify. If you ask anyone that knows me, they'll tell you how much I love order, lists, planning, processes, understanding, and CLARITY. My shadow Sparktype, the Advisor, is a close second and something I am called to do in order to enable my primary Sparktype as an Essentialist. Being the Advisor is coaching, mentoring, and developing relationships and trust. This was the cup that wasn't being fulfilled in my life at that point. I now needed to find something that fulfilled both sides of me. Ironically, as I was seeking clarity within myself, I discovered that my core purpose **"is to help bring clarity to others as a guide"**.

What followed was an extensive search of multiple industries, career paths and practices globally in order to narrow down to an option that could fulfil both sides of my purpose. The result was business architecture. As a relatively emerging practice in Australia, I didn't know what was involved in this role, but it piqued my interest enough to search for a course to learn more. Unfortunately, the courses locally didn't feel like the right fit, so I researched virtually led courses when I discovered a practitioner on the other side of the world, in Canada.

Driven by the energy that emerged because of purpose alignment, I found myself sitting in my office late at night, glued to my laptop with the rest of the house, silent and dark. My family was fast asleep, but my brain was lit up like a Christmas tree - I knew this was it! With every new concept, my business architect trainer stepped through, I smiled and nodded like the Cheshire cat. These practices and concepts were like music to my ears. The glue and map facilitated clarity at all levels of an organisation. I liken it to a blueprint of a building or a city - these blueprints bring together multiple disciplines with a shared vision: engineers, builders, electricians, plumbers, and city planners, enabling them to execute their separate work plans to bring about the outcome. It also allows them to understand when they intersect with other trades and when they need to work together. With business architecture blueprints, it can achieve the same behaviour and outcome by mapping an organisation's value-driven processes, capabilities, information, and relationships. Helping leaders understand the impact of their investment and strategy execution decisions. This is a relevant and much-needed practice to support our current and future leaders. Imagine if the teams under these leaders also had access to the exact shared blueprint in which they could align their design and execution of the strategy.

So now what? I found my clarity on my 'what'; now, I needed to find my 'how'. How do I find my way into a role that is not mainstream in Australia without experience in the job title? I knew I needed help from outside of my normal circle, so I took on mentors in a wholehearted way. It was not cheap, but it was an investment in my future self, so I tightened the belt and made it happen. I decided to get one for each Sparketype.

To develop my *Essentialist* skills within business architecture, I asked my business architecture trainer, Navid from Archist (archist.com), to be my coach and mentor - to ensure I could continue to develop my skills and leverage his many years of experience. We also shared the passion for creating impactful visual Blueprints to facilitate robust conversations and decision-making. For the shadow Sparketype, the *Advisor*, I worked with a more holistic communications coach. At a women's speaking event, I met Melanie from Speaking Styles (speakingstyles.com.au) and connected with her instantly. The art of communication is often taken for granted and is a neglected skill in many aspects of our life. This has made a significant difference in how I approach any personal or business-oriented interactions.

I've since had the opportunity to apply business architecture practices and blueprinting across the not-for-profit, Australian Government and private sector. I've been able to map and learn about the different ecosystems, systemic barriers and patterns that stand in the way of change. I've also learnt and experienced the reality of the daily challenges leaders are facing in today's environment; personal lives, health, COVID-19, mental well-being, and volatile economic, political, and social conditions. During these times, decision-making can be reactive, flux in and out of crisis mode, but this is not sustainable, and we need structure to help us move and look forward.

I wanted to be able to invest my skills and resources, collaborate with other passionate change-makers and work towards a future where business architecture techniques are standard practice in how we create meaningful change in our organisations and communities. So my big hairy audacious goal (BHAG) is to transfer knowledge and practices of blueprinting through stories and speaking engagements, reaching visionary leaders all around the world. This led to the inception of my business **moore2it.com.au**. She is my new second baby, and as part of this new endeavour, I have developed a holistic approach which is an amalgamation of my practical experience across multiple industries and sectors, analyst disciplines and the business architecture framework. The approach enables anyone in the organisation to move through blueprint development, starting small and empowering anyone to benefit from these practices.

Change starts with visionary leaders who can imagine a future that is currently not here yet. My mission is to help visionary leaders bring their vision to life. Doing this work lights me up from the inside out, my eyes wide, my energy harnessed. All my focus is laser pointed on uncovering clarity for individuals, teams, projects, programs, departments, or organisations. I live for the moment of clarity in people's eyes, that light bulb moment, when they raise their finger to say 'aha' and have a little sparkle in their eye brighter than before.

I turn up every day for my clients, looking for our next opportunity to bring clarity to drive strategic change. I have since had opportunities to help others find their clarity of purpose, including career events for business analysts. Business architecture is an ideal path for people with an analytical mindset who enjoy the broader strategic picture.
How are you going with answering the question I asked you at the beginning?

How important is having clarity in your life and work? Are you ready to find your purpose?

My wish for you is that you can take some tangible steps to create clarity in your life, business, or workplace. So follow me on LinkedIn and collect your free blueprint templates from my website. I have also started a series of short videos inspired by my now 4-year-old daughter, who asks me about 20 times a day, "do you know what?" followed by always insightful learnings or facts from her day.

I will forever be grateful to my family, friends, colleagues, mentors, and leaders who have been with me throughout all my journeys, always taking time to listen, encourage and give me faith to follow the path to clarity. Nothing worthwhile is done in a vacuum, and I would not be the person I am without you all. I am filled with love and gratitude.

About the Author

Susie Moore is a Certified Business Architecture (CBA)® Practitioner who is passionate about helping visionary leaders bring their strategies to life through the process of blueprinting. Susie has over 16 years of experience across many industries, including oil, gas, mining, banking, government agencies, utilities, entertainment, and not-for-profit.

A Malaysian-born Kiwi living in Australia, she loves mystery series, karaoke, rugby union, heart-warming food, and embarking on adventures big and small.

She lives for the moment of clarity when faces are illuminated and the energy shifts from resisting to leaning in. Susie has garnered respect from many leaders and teams she has served, past and present, with a reputation for guiding through complexity.

Email: susie@moore2it.com.au
LinkedIn: linkedin.com/in/susiemoore06
Website: moore2it.com.au

Voices of Impact

Lorrayne Robbinz

I was a good Catholic girl from a good Catholic family with a run-of-the-mill upbringing, without much affection from parents, with two younger sisters until I was 11 years of age. When my little brother was born just before, I went away to six years of Catholic girls boarding school, to which I'd won a 6-year scholarship. Having gained First Place in my country diocese, and to which I had no idea what that entailed, I just loved learning!

All I knew was I was leaving home (2 hours away) at 12 years of age to practically fend for myself from then on. I was only returning home three times a year in the holidays to a family that seemed to keep growing further and further apart from me. Not only in the distance but feeling even more different. I'd already felt like I didn't belong even in my own family, but now I was going to be different from all my friends, and I was the only person I knew who went to private school. So the pressure was upon me to not only survive this new life that seemed foreign to me but also to perform well and live up to everyone else's expectations.

I think I became the 'class clown', which wasn't always taken well…especially by the hard-working, studious girls I'd beaten in the competition to get there…and cover up my shyness, fear, and my overwhelming homesickness. But, there were some fun times in the later years. I recall doing a solo performance in a school drama night once, reciting a poem in about 7 different characters. I also taught myself the guitar and was part of a 'Folk Group' with some friends, who had the opportunity of being the entertainment at some local events, like Flower Shows and Horse Race meetings. I seemed to be a different person when performing too!

This sense of humour and fun I'd found proved to keep me in good stead throughout my life in all sorts of circumstances, most, fortunately, and I have forever been so grateful for that! However, I realise now it was the beginning of covering up my true feelings and putting on a brave face and bottling things up inside to my detriment, involving my health.

I met my childhood sweetheart at 14 on one of my holidays back home. It was a pen-pal type of relationship until I left boarding school at 17. For a while after that as well, because my Mum had arranged a job in a bank and accommodation in a hostel, again run by nuns just like boarding school but now in the big city! My family still lived in a small country town with no job prospects, and my Mum wasn't going to be embarrassed with any of her children on the 'dole'. Especially after attending Private School, so I was packed up to leave home, away from my family, to fend for myself once again. My life was being arranged for me once again, whether I liked it or not. I would rather have been in the air force or a teacher of some kind, but that wasn't to be. I had no say in anything, once again!

My boyfriend ended up in the city with me after a couple of years when he obtained a great position as being the youngest acting-Postmaster in the southern suburbs of the city. I had admired him from the first time I met him; he had three jobs to help make a better life for himself from a dysfunctional family life he had endured. He was the local postman during the day when not serving on the counter and/or studying to be a Postmaster and the night-shift telephonist. A Postmaster's job in those days was considered very prestigious, especially in the country, and held in high regard, and you were usually supplied with a house for your family with a good salary. He had great plans already to be a great husband, a great dad, and a great provider for his own family.

Despite my parents thinking my boyfriend was not good enough for me, I was determined to marry him because I was so in love and believed I was doing the right thing for myself, not thinking of the pressure I was placing myself under to make it succeed. All I knew was my dream to marry and be a mum was coming true!

My life seemed complete when we had our first child, a daughter, at 23, but that's when things began to change. My husband changed whenever he drank; it seemed he began to have anger outbursts, sometimes taking it out on me, but each time he was sorry. I thought it was because of the stress of becoming pregnant too early before we had our own home, and I'd given up work, so he was carrying the load of working three jobs. So it was with great internal turmoil that I put our child into daycare and returned to work when she was 12 months old. I had thought that would help and change things back to the way they were, and I thought I'd blocked out most of that time. Still, I do remember a few times having to cover bruises to serve customers at work and my workmates offering me a haven for a time, only to return to my husband with promises for it to stop.

Things were much better for some time, especially when we had bought our little home in a country town until our daughter was about 3. Then, I remembered he had hit me in front of her; he hadn't even been drinking this time! That shocked me so much that I instinctually packed for my daughter and me, and before I knew it, we had landed on my parents' doorstep! I don't even know how I made the 3-hour trip. It must have been bad for me to do that because I was determined to make a success of my relationship, and yet I felt like a failure with my parents being proven right all along. However, within about a month, I was back in that relationship for several reasons.

One was my parents weren't going to have a divorce in their family, having said I'd 'made my bed so I must lie in it' and to get myself back to my husband where I belong now. Surprisingly my husband turned up in person apologising to me in front of my parents and apologised to them for treating me badly and promised he'd never hit me again. I thought it took guts to do all that, taking responsibility, especially to my dad. I was blown away to see him so gaunt and frail, having lost over a stone in weight. I also thought if my parents were prepared to give him another chance, I should at least do the same. He never did hit me again, but there were still the angry bouts that still frightened me and made me concerned for him; as to what was troubling him, all I could think was his upbringing, where he'd told me that he and his brothers were beaten with fence palings. However, how was I supposed to deal with that except to wait till he was himself again and suggest he get help.

He didn't, though, until…15 years had passed, with the good times outweighing the bad, including having two more beautiful children, a girl and a boy, 18 months apart. Without going through the whole 18 months of hell we endured, my daughter didn't come home from school one Friday afternoon, with her brother telling me she was presumably helping her teacher with the coming weekend's class camp. Still, I'd not heard anything officially until after my third call to the school asking where my daughter was, only to be told by someone in the office I didn't know that "she has accused her dad of molesting her and police are interviewing her"! I almost fell to the floor, stunned, paralysed, shocked to have that blurted out to me as if it was nothing! My whole world disintegrated at that moment, and it never really recovered. This is what my self-published book is about, and because of the sensitive, taboo subject, I needed to write it under a pen name to try and protect my family again. While it was a kind of apology to my three children for being in a zombie state most of their lives following the devastation and injustices, while trying to survive, but also trying to help so many other victims like us and try to change laws and society's perceptions.

Yes, I've written a book, but it took over 20 years to do it, and I have self-published it on the insistence of one of my counsellors. Who suggested it to be a great learning curve for all other counsellors from which to learn. Due to my speaking out for lots of other victims and having a different view and perception about it all, with the way I dealt with my family's circumstances. My aim was to get help for all of us at the time, but none of us got the right counselling and help that we should have because it was all put in the too-hard basket for everyone concerned, especially the so-called professionals. My young 12-year-old daughter had been grilled by police for four hours and taken from me to a strange place, like she was in the wrong, and has never really spoken about it ever since!

It's taken me a lot of time, help, and treatments on my own steam to at least be able to talk about it all without becoming too emotional anymore. I believe that no matter how many books we read, how many courses we take, how many therapies we undergo, or how much help we get. It's ultimately up to us to do the hard yards/work to recover because we are all individuals who have experienced different things. I've realised that even within a small family unit, we can only help each other to a certain extent, but even though the family devastation happened to all of us, we still cannot understand or comprehend what it was like for each other, because it affected us all so differently. Ultimately, the loss of TRUST may be the thread that joins the whole family together, but it was also broken within us in various degrees of damage.

Because abuse/molestation is a cyclical thing, the main abuser would have had his trust broken by someone to be reliving/replaying his abuse; his direct physical victim had her trust broken by her own dad, someone she loved, the abuser's eldest child had her trust broken because she couldn't believe her dad whom she loved would do such a thing, his youngest and only son had his trust broken because he loved his dad/his best mate and was too young to understand why his dad had to leave the family, while his wife, loving partner of nearly 25 years, had her trust broken because how could she not know and how could he hurt her so much, knowing how much they loved one another and up until the devastation thought they had a great relationship who usually told each other everything.

All this reasoning has been going around in my head ever since, and the reason why all the family needs help is because of the different and various after-effects, and the reason why I had to teach my kids that 'you can always LOVE someone, but you don't have to LIKE what they do', especially when in our circumstance the abuser was my kid's dad...the other 50% of them. Also, because of the statistics that one in every three girls and one in every seven boys are abused by someone they know and trust to annihilate and punish the victims, abusers are victimising the victims all over again; hence, when that happens, the victim's self-esteem is shot to pieces, and they can end up hating themselves, ending up on drugs and in jail, especially too when the young victims are usually the ones who inform on their own abusers because they just want the abuse to stop but not make trouble for anyone. I also believe that some older victims report their abuse years after in anger that has built up over the years because of how they truly believe their abuser ruined their whole lives. In fact, from my own experience, I feel when you harbour anger for the people or things people do to you, you're still giving them power over your life and still feeling abused until you can learn to forgive them and take your own power and control back. That's one of the ways that helped me to take my own life back and learn from the reasons why things happened in my family; until then, I was going crazy.

Only just recently have I realised that I was fooling myself by thinking I was healed because I'd written my book and had it out there helping other people feel like they weren't alone and that they can survive anything like I'd promised myself'…I started believing what all my loved ones and well-wishers kept telling me that I had it all out of my system, and I should well and truly be on the mend and ready to power ahead. BUT…It all kept gnawing at me, even more so, and I was wondering why I continued to wallow in the past and why it was still affecting me. The word that came to mind was SHAME! No matter what you do to help heal yourself, you need to forgive yourself of any guilt from the past. Because it's believed 'you can only act on your level of awareness at the time, and there needs to be the unveiling of shame. The shame comes from society's eyes and the way they treat taboo subjects, all the name-calling that doesn't pertain to most abusers because they have usually been victims themselves at one stage in this horrid cycle. Not realising that it's a society that's keeping this taboo subject underground and secret because no one feels safe in talking about it! It's the shame that keeps us under our pennames and face masks! It angers me that society still has this warped sense of Christianity, treating victims as lepers; nothing has changed!

That's why I'm so grateful to have been given this Chapter to write under my own name, to enable me to advertise my own book under this safe 'umbrella' to those who may like to read it to help them feel supported, understood, and not alone, at least…

"I Just Want My Old Daddy Back … From a Mother's Perspective"
…By Kimberley Jane
Self-Published with Balboa Press (Australian Branch of Hay House Publishing)
Purchased through me. Contact details at the end!

Another passion of mine, which helped keep me sane all these years, is Numerology, a study of people's strengths and weaknesses they are born with to use on their earthly journey, obtained mainly from their Birthdates alone.

One of my mottos is SIBKIS…See It Big, Keep It Simple! This is the way I've been taught Numerology, and this is the way I teach it. My aim is to introduce as many people as possible to Numerology to be able to find themselves again through their date of birth. I love Numerology because it's all about factual numbers; your Birthdate can never change, and numbers never lie, so you can always rely on the energies we are each born with. Each number has certain energy; the numbers we are born with are our strengths, which we are given to work WITH, and the numbers we are missing are our weaknesses, which we are given to work ON, with the aim to ultimately live to our full potential and to our true selves.

Numerology is a way of keeping track of yourself and living your best life. I especially love doing Family Grid Pages. Have you ever thought you don't belong in your certain family, or why do you get on better with some people and not others? Numerology can help with that. I only wish I'd learnt about Numerology much earlier because it could have prevented some family rifts, for one thing, and I would have known myself better for longer and maybe not made so many mistakes. We all wish we could have learnt from our good times instead of our not-so-good ones, and then we'd all be more optimistic, perhaps.

One of the main reasons I love doing families is for them to get to know one another's true natures and not the masks we wear sometimes and the things we bottle up to avoid conflicts that all can cause underlying resentment and anger for some. If we really know our own families and the energies they are born with, we can learn why each of us is in our lives by finding out who is supposed to teach us what and vice-versa. That way, we can all learn to understand and accept each other for our true selves, not the 'selves' we sometimes present ourselves to others. To know the truth keeps us more in tune with one another and improves our communication is the basis for all great relationships, no matter who they're with.

Until now, Numerology has only really been a hobby for me doing friends and family; however, I've realised it's become my true purpose, my more positive way of showing people how they can counsel themselves! After all, we're the ones who must live with and love ourselves. So, I'm hoping to create a platform for myself soon to continue my purpose in the best way possible!

About the Author

Lorrayne Robbinz is a self-published author and successful businesswoman. She is a woman, grandmother, fighter of injustices, and importantly an 'in-between'. A surviving mother of an abused child and wife of a perpetrator!

Because of her struggles to overcome her family's devastation, she has been described as courageous, persistent, resilient, with integrity, strength, empathy, determination and pure spirit, a survivor to enable her to help others! Numerology made a huge impact on her survival, so her passion for her 'hobby' has become her 'purpose' in life... to teach others to survive in a more positive way by getting to know their own strengths again! Forgiveness also helps her thrive rather than just survive!

Lorrayne also loves walks on the beach, writing, and enjoying quality time with her children, grandchildren, family, and friends! I can be contacted by texting my phone or email (I only answer calls from phone numbers I know)

Phone: 0400 501 957
Email: lorraynerobbinz@bigpond.com

Dr Libby Roesner

A Cooee from Women in the Bush

I am both a city girl and a country girl.

I've had the unique experience of living in each of these 'worlds' for half of my life. I consider myself to be a bridge of understanding between country and city living in Australia. I have a pretty good perspective of what each place entails, and I have a strong understanding of the blessings and failings of both.

I know that supporting rural communities, making wise food choices, and conscious decisions of what we purchase and who we employ will make a huge impact on the health and prosperity of our rural landscape, our environment, our nation, and our whole planet.

In this chapter, I want to convey how important it is for us to buy local and support rural and regional areas. Rural areas are the blood force of our country, and without them, we wouldn't be able to feed or cloth ourselves without relying on imports from other countries (*read China*). Women are a critical factor in maintaining small communities, and we need strong, thriving communities to ensure the continued prosperity of our food and fibre production systems.

Farmers are the guardians of our landscapes, and their management decisions can affect the quality of our natural resources (*read soil, water, air, and ecosystems*). A strong, caring, and prosperous rural community that can support our farming landholders is critical. A regenerative effort in our agricultural systems can transform the ecosystem and ensure the continued health of our environment.

I believe that each one of us can make a difference. All we need is to make a thoughtful stand on what we truly value and ensure that we follow through with good choices *every time* we go shopping because what we buy and who we chose to employ will have massive consequences on the future of our rural communities, the prosperity of our nation and the health of our whole planet.

Why am I Supporting Rural Women

My desire to support rural women was borne from my journey through post-graduate studies, agricultural research, living and working in a small rural community, running a farming business, as well as volunteering and supporting community initiatives, organisations, and events.

The nature of every woman, wife and mother is to nurture and support their families and the people around them. When rural women are given an opportunity to bloom where they are, there is a ripple effect, and all around her bloom. This means that providing opportunities for rural women to thrive will always have a positive impact on their communities and the rural environment as well.

As a wife and mother, I know that in a family, most of the household purchasing decisions come down to us. We are often the ones who make the final call when buying groceries, clothing, housewares, and gifts. This means that women can have a great influence on our planet's future simply by altering our daily purchasing choices.

We can choose to make a positive impact every time we put something in our shopping carts. We can also have an influence on our families, our children and our friends. We can talk about the importance of making wise purchasing decisions, and together we can alter the state of our communities and our environment.

When you live in a remote regional community, you know firsthand the devastating effects of what happens when people do not shop locally or support their local businesses. The businesses eventually close, and each time that happens, people leave town, and the community shrinks.

I'm sure that you realise that the same thing happens every time you buy cheap imported goods. In Australia, many manufacturing businesses are under imminent threat of bankruptcy and closure because they can't compete with overseas businesses with their much lower labour prices. Many Australian factories and companies have closed or moved their manufacturing arms overseas to remain competitive.

The same can be said for the trend of offshoring our labour force. The current swing to the "gig" economy has created a competitive space for providing remote skills and acquiring cheap labour from overseas countries. The money that would otherwise go to provide incomes to Australian residents and taxes for our country is sent overseas.

Rural, remote, and regional women are well known for being industrious. There are many examples of creative women who establish their own cottage industries and businesses from their own homes or farms to support their families' incomes. Making jams, candles, and clothing are just the tip of the iceberg.

Online platforms such as "Buy from the Bush" and "Spend with Us" have an enormous array of quality products that you can purchase, and most of them are homemade by rural woman. These successful online platforms invite city people to connect with them and buy their charming homewares and gifts. What you will find are beautiful, unique, and stylish products of high quality, made locally. I love their products, and I strongly encourage you to jump on these platforms and have a look when considering your next homeware or gift purchase.

Rural, regional, and remote women are incredibly strong, determined, and resilient; however, in terms of opportunities available to them, they have always had a huge disadvantage from their city cousins. Finding professional employment in rural areas can be very difficult, and this is why so many children of country people end up leaving the bush and living in urban areas. Of course, every time this happens, the rural community shrinks some more.

I experienced this personally, and it led to me using my very wide skill base to remain employable. So often, I would see highly skilled young women with amazing degrees and qualifications forced to leave, or to do work in menial jobs, just to be employable in their towns. We need to find a way to solve this problem, or our towns will be diminished further. As women acquire higher qualifications and skills, they need to have more options to work from rural areas.

A Virtual Solution

One way I have proudly supported rural women has been by co-founding a business specifically for encouraging skilled rural women to offer their professional services online, and for businesses everywhere to find and hire these women to provide virtual assistant (or VA) services. As hiring a rural woman brings money into rural regions, this allows them to support their families and stay in their communities and thrive.

'The Virtual Cooee' is an online employment hub for businesses to connect with rural and regional virtual assistants and freelancers. If you are looking for support in your business, whether you are city or country-based, consider looking here to find a skilled Australian woman to support you.

My business partner, Emily Sinderberry, and I are proud to provide this platform to try and address this issue for rural women. Together, we have created a marketplace where skilled Australian rural and regional women can offer their services as Virtual Assistants and be connected to rural, regional, and metropolitan businesses to be paid for their services.

Our idea in creating this platform was to inspire women in small communities to become Virtual Assistants and help them to provide them with an income source, especially when they can't find suitable roles in their local regions. We wanted to help change the course of small communities that often struggle to find people to live and stay there. We believe that providing this platform gives a massive opportunity for isolated women as it gives them access to a world of employment and income that they can tap into.

Finding remote work as a Virtual Assistant opens a whole new world of professional achievement and growth for women regardless of where they live. We believe that we can improve the lives and well-being of rural women by fuelling an environment where women who have ideas and skills also have the opportunity to develop themselves and provide services from wherever they are.

The focus of The Virtual Cooee is to provide businesses with access to online freelance workers who are skilled rural women like myself. The platform is for anyone in the business community who needs administration or any specialised support online. The definition of a VA and the types of services on offer are endless – if a service doesn't require you to physically be in the room, and you can do it online, you can offer it as a virtual assistant.

The opportunity exists for any business, big or small, to outsource and be supported by a skilled rural woman rather than 'offshoring' their outsourcing to a cheap overseas labour force. The type of work is often ad hoc or project-based. This is often the perfect support for small business owners who can't afford to put on full-time or even a part-time person yet.

If you are in a position where you need some administrative or other support, please don't hesitate to jump online at look at our Hub. It's free to join, and it's free to post your listings there. Whether you are wanting to post a job request and find a rural VA, or you are a rural or regional woman, and you want to post your skills or service offering, please join our community and get involved. You can find our employment Hub at: www.thevirtualcooe.com.au.

We'd love it if you would consider supporting rural and regional women as we know that the flow-on effects will help their whole communities to thrive and keep our regional areas prosperous and our whole environment healthy.

How did I get here?

I grew up in Cremorne - Sydney, NSW but always loved country life. My family had a small farm in Oberon, NSW, and I always loved escaping the city to find my inner calm in the bush. I studied Agricultural Science at The University of Sydney, majored in Soil Science, and completed a PhD in Soil Physics.

Finally, after 25 years of schooling, university studies and fast-paced city living, I left the "big smoke" for a "tree change". I went to take up an agricultural research position in a small country town called Condobolin, 6 hours away in the centre of New South Wales (the population was about 2000 people) – I figured I was going to Woop Woop.

My Woop Woop experience was only meant to be a 13-month stint in the bush to complete a short-term research project for the Department of Primary Industries (DPI) before I returned home to my familiar city. And yet, what I did not know was that I would end up spending the next 25 years of my life enraptured by the pull of this little country town, its people, its rural and natural landscape, and all it entails. What I found in Condobolin was a remote community with heart and some of the most delightful, hardworking, fun, honest, and authentic people I'd ever met.

What I didn't know was that I'd fall in love with my own charming cowboy, get married and start a family in this little town. I didn't realise then that I would become so deeply involved with the sports, music, education, business, arts, crafts, and environment of the region. I couldn't have comprehended that as an outsider, I'd become so involved in all these organisations and that I would get so entangled with living in this small rural community that I'd feel like I'd become a part of its very fabric.

When I came to study the pastures, crops, and soils of this region, I had no idea that I'd also end up buying a farm and working hard to generate a living off it. I was excited to be finally experiencing firsthand what I'd learnt in my Ag degree. However, I didn't count on the wild extremes of desiccating droughts, devastating floods, immense dust storms, severe hailstorms, and insane plagues of locusts and mice.

I also didn't realise that I'd be so inspired by the regenerative movement that I'd want to transform the agricultural practices of the region and beyond to build better soils, grow high-quality, nutritious food, enhance the natural environment, and create a healthier future for everyone.

My hubby Rob and I bought our 330-acre run-down irrigation property on the Lachlan River in the middle of a drought in 2008. We transformed it into a thriving and healthy, diverse and profitable farm. We grew dryland pastures and irrigated crops, we bred merino sheep and had cattle on agistment. We also constructed a series of paddocks and stables and built a horse-spelling complex where we were able to feed and look after horses for others. We also specialised in growing irrigated lucerne and oaten hay for the horse market. It was a lot of hard work, plenty of sweat and tears, but we managed to make it work and created a lifestyle for our children that was fantastic.

Bringing up children in the bush is such a joy; they have space and freedom to roam and explore the natural environment. They gain incredible life skills riding motorbikes, horses, boats, fishing, and camping, and they learn to drive farm vehicles and interact with farm animals from a young age. They also gain an amazing sense of practical creativity; they'd go into the shed to build things for fun, fix them, and solve problems. They weren't so interested in screens when they were young because outside their front door, they could roam free and create their own adventures.

While I was in Condobolin, I worked in various roles; I started as a full-time soil scientist and pasture researcher for the DPI and later, when I had babies to look after and no relatives nearby, I had to find part-time roles, as I needed to balance my career with mothering and helping to run a farm business. Despite being highly qualified with a university degree and PhD, it was extremely difficult for me to find any flexible, professional work in Condobolin. The DPI provided some casual work for a while, but then funding ran out, and opportunities for using my professional skills with other employers just weren't there.

In my now-evolving career, I had to improvise and use the width of my skill base to find work. I eventually found part-time work as a TAFE Teacher, I began teaching business administration and bookkeeping using the skills I'd gained in our business. I also volunteered where I could with the various organisations and community groups I was involved with. I supported the preschool, primary school, Little Athletics & Karate club, the Pipeband, Arts Council, Agricultural Show and Farming Systems group, among others. I was proficient in taking minutes, contributing to, and overseeing meetings, and providing whatever technical, creative or admin support I could. I even managed to establish my own side-hustle designing Excel spreadsheets and doing graphic design work to assist various local individuals and groups.

In 2016, I landed another part-time role working as a Landcare Coordinator; in this role, I was able to use some of my agricultural knowledge and delve into the wonders of natural resource management and my passion for the environment. It was in this position that I activated the local movement toward regenerative agriculture in the region. I also started many other initiatives, including bringing 'Boomerang Bags' to Condobolin and instigating the 'Primary Schools Environment Day', an event designed to bring environmental experts and school children together to learn from each other. I organised bird-watching breakfast events and ran an art exhibition bringing together local artists and photographers to promote birds of the grey box ecosystem.

In 2019, I humbly received an Australia Day Award as the Environmental Citizen of the Lachlan Shire. As you can see, I had become very involved, and I really felt like a part of the fabric of the town.

In 2020, the Covid-19 virus brought everything in my little community and the world to a stop. Our schools were closed, our sporting events were cancelled, our community events were postponed, many businesses and workplaces were quarantined, and the Australian borders were shut down from the rest of the world.

It was a time to stay home, and it brought on a period of deep reflection. It was time to concentrate on our family and home/farm life and think about where we were heading and where we wanted to go in the future. Remarkably, it was the very first time I had truly comprehended just how entangled and absorbed my family and I had become with so many of the activities and organisations in our local community, our very busy lives had just seemed normal. Now that everything had stopped and we were free of all our community commitments, it felt like we needed a change.

It was the 5th of May 2020 when we made the unimaginable and totally radical family decision to leave Condobolin. We realised that the pandemic had provided us with a very rare opportunity to pull up our deep roots and look for another future for our family and particularly for educating our two rapidly growing teenage children who were at the local high school. So, we decided to sell our farm and to go travelling in a caravan and find a new place to live and educate our children. The very next day, we called the local real-estate agent and organised to put our farm on the market.

At the end of October that year, we sold the farm, and we drove out of our beloved property, "Nagiruoh", for the final time. We headed out of Condobolin towing our fifth-wheeler caravan, all set to begin a family adventure and start a new life – somewhere!

About the Author

Dr Libby Roesner is a mother of two, soil scientist, ex-farmer, entrepreneur, virtual assistant, and business owner. She and her husband, Rob Hourigan and their children, Patrick and Hayley Hourigan, now live in Hervey Bay, Queensland. Together they operate a caravan storage business, and Dr Libby runs a digital platform with her co-founder Emily Sinderberry. The Virtual Cooee is an online marketplace where you can find rural and regional women looking to provide their valued professional skills and services 'virtually'.

Dr Libby has a passion for helping rural women; she loves to help business owners who are stuck or need support in learning how to work online. She has developed systems and training to help businesses get set up and find suitable support from virtual assistants. She encourages collaboration between rural businesswomen to create win-win working relationships enabling everyone to work in their zone of genius.

Email: libby@libbyroesner.com
Website: www.thevirtualcooee.com.au
Social media: @thevirtualcooee

Voices of Impact

Vicki Tate

Believe in Your Dreams

As a 4-year-old, I had a dream I was going to become a nurse. I knew it! No amount of persuasion from my parents and grandparents was going to sway me. Both my mother and Grandmother were well-accomplished stenographers and clerical staff. They knew office skills would be useful no matter what career path I chose. But I was determined. I did the research to find the best training hospital in Brisbane and discovered what was needed to be accepted for enrolment as a student nurse.

I was accepted into the Royal Brisbane Hospital Cadet Nursing course in September 1971. I loved every minute of my new life. As a C grade student at school, I was achieving 100% and A gradings on all my assignments. This was the life for me!

All meals for staff and patients were prepared in the hospital kitchen. They were transported to the wards in Bain-Marie carts. Unbeknown to us, on one of my shifts, the food warmer was leaking hot water onto the floor. My feet went flying from under me, and in slow motion, my bottom crashed into the polished cement floor. The thud reverberated right through my being.

My flying feats were not complete; three months later, once

again, support from the ground disappeared while on ice skates as I turned to admire some figure skaters practising in the centre of the rink. Before I could gather any sense of what was happening, I was gasping for breath, and my neck was in the grip of pain. For three days, my equilibrium was completely "off balance".

Little did I know these two incidents would shape my world. For 16 years, I sought pain relief from massage therapists so I could continue working as a Registered Nurse. The therapy did relieve some of the burning, gnawing pain to a tolerable level, so I could perform at work. The home was a different matter. Insomnia, mood swings with fatigue and exhaustion were constant companions.

Eventually, the stress in my neck became too much, and I received another injury at work. This time, I tore my biceps in my left arm. I was also diagnosed with a partial tear in the muscles of my right arm and tendonitis. Now with both arms unable to do simple tasks like open a drip bottle, make a bed, or dispense medication, the hospital decided I was to be dismissed.

That day was devastating! I had a mortgage, a teenage son, a truckload of pain, no income, no support, and no idea where to turn.

My massage therapist referred me to an osteopath who treated my injuries with gentle movements and some painless 'home exercises'. Within three visits, I was vastly improved. I wanted to help others with this gentle and supportive technique. After inquiring, I discovered she was using Ortho-Bionomy. I had never heard of it and wanted to know more. She invited me to an introduction demonstration with one of the international instructors.

Suddenly, it all made sense. I signed up for the weekend course to help myself, my friends, and my family. The workshop spoke to me at a deep cellular level. I immediately decided this was the new career path for me and committed to studying for five years to become an Advance Practitioner of Ortho-Bionomy.

My friends were incredibly supportive as they felt the changes and improvements in their bodies and range of movement immediately. This was all the encouragement I needed. A naturopath became my principal referrer, and my practice began to grow. The trauma from my injuries was resolved, and I was able to return to nursing part-time to help support my family and financial commitments during this emerging stage. My private practice continued to flourish. I began to reach out in various ways to help members of the community reduce their pain and stress.

One of my clients suggested I approach the Queensland Ambulance Service 000 desk to give 15-minute sessions to the operators who were incredibly stressed and often complained of pain during their long shifts. These sessions were fast-paced and rewarding.

One day, an angry young woman came for her 15-minute appointment. She had suffered pain since she was 12 years old, and "nothing worked'. It was obvious she had significant scoliosis (sideways curvature of the spine) in her upper and lower back. There wasn't a lot I could do in 15 minutes. So, I explored positions of comfort with her and showed her a movement her boyfriend might be able to help her with during the week when her back becomes distressingly painful.

I didn't expect to see her again. The next week, she booked an appointment for her entire lunch break. I was surprised, to say the least! When I enquired what had prompted this longer appointment, she said that after the previous session, she felt comfortable for the first time in over 14 years, and she wanted more.

I was encouraged by her results and began seeking out scoliosis clients. In 2010, I started scoliosis and back pain relief workshops called "Spine Unwind". People reported their migraines disappearing, improved movement, reduced pain in almost every joint and improved energy at the end of a few hours of learning relaxing movements. The Ortho-Bionomy Association of Australia asked me to deliver a Scoliosis Strategies workshop to assist other practitioners to find comfort, increased range of movement and pain relief for their clients.

For 24 years, I have never been bored with Ortho-Bionomy. It was a match made in heaven for me and my unique skill set. I have acute observational skills and attention to detail, refined tactile senses, a curiosity about how the body mechanics work and 51 years of nursing background. I was hearing many of my clients report relief from symptoms that had plagued them for decades, even though they had sought treatment from many other modalities and practitioners.

A colleague I met at a workshop invited me to teach relaxation and meditation techniques to a group at Vietnam Veterans Counselling Service (VVCS). I jumped at the opportunity even though I was tentative about being in a room with 12 men diagnosed with Post Traumatic Stress Disorder (PTSD). I wasn't sure if the techniques I was teaching them were going to be appreciated or effective. Yet, I had seen miraculous results with my private clients. I did know when the emotions and psychology are challenged, and the body often holds the key to calm and reason. The next day, the facilitator called and asked if I would return for another session. That lead to many years of presenting somatic, breath and body awareness techniques to the veterans and their wives at the Spring Hill office and during the weeklong residentials.

I relocated often, and as a result, I had to restart my practice every time I moved. Some clients followed me from Brisbane Northside to Stanthorpe, to the Sunshine Coast, back to Brisbane Southside and more recently, to the Moreton Bay region 40 km north of Brisbane.

For 20 years, every time I moved my practice or there was an economic downturn, I would return to nursing as my back-up-plan. I called nursing my 'Money Tree'. My heart always belonged to Ortho-Bionomy and my clients who sought me out. With nursing, I was able to contribute a wealth of knowledge and compassion to my patients while teaching carers and other registered staff through the art of nursing. These skills were appreciated and valued. Consequently, nursing work was easy for me to find.

In January 2020, while working weekends at a local aged care facility, I received a call from the care staff that someone had fallen, and I was needed "urgently". I responded immediately. As I turned the corner in my haste, I felt a searing pain in my right ankle. Suddenly, I was unable to walk or weight bare. I began to sweat and feel faint with the pain. An ankle injury I had sustained about four years earlier had started to become troublesome. My podiatrist had designed supports, and I was wearing corrective shoes as recommended, but these measures were not enough to protect me from the horrific injury I sustained this time.

During the next couple of months, I did the rounds with a Physiotherapist, X-ray and my GP before being referred to the Lower Limb Orthopaedic Surgeon. When she reviewed my CT scans, she put her head in her hands and remained silent for what seemed like an eternity. She was straight up with me and declared it was a terrible injury which had damaged two joints of the ankle. The surgical option was not suitable for my bones. She suggested rest, an ugly splint to totally support my lower leg and ankle, front and back, and pain management. Only to return when I couldn't stand it any longer, and then we would talk about surgical options again.

At 64, I was washed up. I couldn't stand or walk. I could only work in my clinic for one hour at a time before needing to have my foot elevated for two-three hours to relieve the swelling and pain. Both of my career paths were shot. I was in grief and felt helpless and hopeless. All the activities I had enjoyed were now out of reach. Gardening was very difficult. Bushwalking was out of the question. Body surfing was a no-go as the movement of the water and sand provided me with no support at all and caused an immense amount of pain.

For two years, I virtually sat on my couch and mourned my previous life. Inside, I still felt young and strong, yet in the physical world, I was weak, dependent, and defeated. Ordinary activities like watering the garden caused me to sweat, limp painfully and become breathless with the slightest amount of exertion. I felt I was a burden on society. The global "pandemic" in March 2020 also contributed to staying isolated at home and not mixing with people who were inspirational and supportive. Zoom calls just didn't do it for me. I was no longer able to see any clients as all face-to-face activities were restricted for almost a year.

I enrolled in several planning days and goal-setting workshops but couldn't finish anything or feel motivated to change my sad life. Although deep down, I wanted my life to look and feel different, I yearned to feel passionate about *anything*, to have the get-up-and-go I used to have when designing courses or giving keynote addresses. All that seemed to be something of the past. I stopped believing in myself. I stopped having faith in my abilities.

Life has a way of happening while we are busy making plans. A conversation with my son was the catalyst for change. He started comparing my lifestyle to my 85-year-old mother, who was starting to demonstrate signs of dementia. That hurt! That conversation dealt a deep blow. My ego and self-respect had a knee-jerk reaction. I realised even though it was hurtful, in part, it was true. I had been waiting for someone to come and rescue me. Within days, I made decisions to stop waiting for someone to come and help, to start living into my purpose and begin moving toward my goals and dreams one step at a time.

Around the same time, during a women's gathering, the idea of starting a Mastermind group was floated. I was very keen. The initial group consisted of six amazing women, all with completely different skills. We met fortnightly for two hours, following the structure in "Think and Grow Rich" by Napoleon Hill. This group was pivotal in my personal development and the advancement of my ideas for the future.

My old pattern of thinking was no one could help me, and I had to do it all myself. I felt like a caterpillar emerging from the chrysalis. The process was exciting and painful at the same time. I decided my work was needed more than ever because nearly everyone was isolated at home, working on the phone, zoom and computer. Even students and teachers were forced to sit behind screens for the whole of the educational day. And I needed help. A lot of help.

The political climate was uncertain, with rolling lockdowns reducing contact and mandates changing daily. I had no confidence that any freedom we were granted would be lasting, as lockdowns seemed to roll out at short notice. The world had shifted to the digital space. Information was shared via screens, podcasts, online courses and zoom calls. This was the way of the future.

I am old school. Not very familiar or literate with computers. I needed to learn new skill sets and take the hands-on work I've been sharing for 25 years and use those skills to teach, support and heal people online. How on earth was I going to do that? So many questions, frustrations, roadblocks, and mishaps were ahead of me.

"Everything you want is outside your comfort zone". I was certainly outside my comfort zone. It was exciting and extremely scary at the same time. I wanted to do what I had been doing for years but present it in a different way and to a different audience.

I was stepping into the role of a true business owner. I was taking my skills and extending them into a bigger community so many more could benefit. I was being asked to write about it, define it, polish it and expose it to people who mattered. People of influence.

The first steps were the most challenging. My fears, doubts and insecurities all rose like a tidal wave. At times I felt swamped, drowning in my own defeating thoughts. None of them were real, yet ever so present and impactful on my self-confidence. I was swept away sometimes, powerlessly floating on the wave of despair.

Slowly, I reached for support and coaching where more was expected of me. I was asked to do more, be more, and give more. Those supportive colleagues and friendships kept me going through the tears and fears. Our Mastermind group proved to be a lifesaver. I could speak my truth and be heard. My coaches guide me through the daunting processes. I couldn't have done it without their experience, prompting and sage advice. The way through was to keep paddling and master small steps before leaping to the next part of the pathway.

Some initial online sessions proved to be surprisingly effective for the participants. One client with a complex and complicated set of symptoms, including vertigo, neck pain, lower back pain, shoulder bursitis and knee pain, reported long-lasting relief from two online sessions. This gave me encouragement to continue exploring the online space with new and continuing clients.

Many times, I was advised to upgrade something small, like my LinkedIn profile. It was suggested it would take about 20 minutes. After many failed attempts to create a new banner, I finally found one that worked for me. It only took three days! Everything seemed to take much longer than expected. Was it me? Was I losing my mind? Or did I simply not understand the platforms? I finally got things done. It was worth it. Persistence paid off!

As my business became more complex, business systems were necessary to save documents and then find them on demand. I was never clerically trained, so my office systems were nonexistent. It was here I needed the most help. A slow and daunting process of reorganising all my documentation, accounting, and bookings into something that supported my clients and myself. Not fun during the changeover. But so worthwhile.

Visitations to self-doubt and overwhelm became almost daily experiences. During this time, my colleagues within the Mastermind Group and coaches were vital to keeping me on track and moving forward, ever so slowly at times.

I have some big goals for the next two years to be achieved or at least partially completed by 2025. I see myself assisting thousands of people with Online Courses specifically designed to alleviate neck and shoulder pain, lower back pain, and upper and lower limb programs, which include strategies to reduce pain and strengthen the knee, shoulder, elbow, and wrist joints. These courses are especially for those tied to a workstation and computer screen for many hours per day or performing repetitive manual tasks.

Another area of passion is to create "Workplace Wellness Programs" for businesses that value their staff and have a desire to offer strategies for workers to remain productive and injury free while executing their work obligations. The programs will consist of practical strategies with movements and stretches that can be performed at the desk or on the job to reduce discomfort and tension, alleviate stress in conflict situations and connect with the central nervous system to receive vital information to maintain and regain wellbeing and calm.

To be able to attain these goals, I will be seeking many speaking opportunities to educate the wider community through clubs, professional organisations, and groups.

When all is said and done, spending quality time with my family is one of my highest values. By serving more people online, I anticipate I will have more time flexibility and be able to visit family and friends more often and travel for work and pleasure within Australia and overseas.

I hope you are inspired to take the plunge and follow your dreams, no matter your age. Creating something you are passionate about, and sharing your experiences with others, can improve the lives of many and leave a legacy for generations to come as you share your wisdom. Living your passion lights a fire within your soul and gives wings to your purpose, and renews energy and vitality in every fibre of your being. It is worth stepping outside your comfort zone.

Never stop Dreaming!

About the Author

Vicki Tate is a Registered Nurse, Advanced Ortho-Bionomy Practitioner and Early Childhood Teacher. She is described as a Body Mechanic, supporting her clients to shift and fine-tune their postural alignment using comfortable movements and awareness of the body's response. Her clients report increased range of movement, reduced pain, swelling and much more!

As a Workplace Wellness Facilitator, she guides participants to experience transformations that expand their awareness of functional movement patterns, strengthen their core, and the ability to "stand on their own two feet" with alignment and ease. Her desire is for humanity to know themselves as self-healing beings that respond and repair with kindness, care, respect, and compassion.

Vicki was born in Brisbane, Queensland, and lives in Moreton Bay, North of Brisbane, on acreage. She loves growing organic food in her 'no-dig' garden and spoiling her 17 chickens.

Email: vicki.bodyspinealign@gmail.com
Facebook: www.facebook.com/bodyandspine
Website: www.bodyspinealign.com.au

Voices of Impact

Danni Vee

Would you like to become a Confident and Grounded Leader in your business and your Life?

Whether it is to create change in the world, in your company or in your life, it all begins within.

To gain unstoppable confidence and feel truly authentic to who you are, it always comes back to self. Love of self. Acceptance of self. Respect for self.

Creating space for self-care, be that through meditation, exercise, nourishing your body better, hanging with your favourite people or reading a book, is essential for women to thrive, for all humans to thrive for that matter. In my programs, I guide women to make simple habit changes so that they can effortlessly create Zen and harmony in a world of chaos. Because let's face it, unless you change your habits, you will return to the day-to-day rut that you're used to because this is your comfort zone. I teach my clients to find comfort in stepping out of their comfort zone and creating a life and legacy of their own design.

It is now time for our adventure to begin together. I am here to guide you through discovering YOU and your complete worthiness and self-belief so you can show up with unstoppable confidence every single time. To understand the importance of balancing your feminine and masculine energy so that you can show up as the Grounded, Confident leader, you dream to be.

I would love for you to begin this chapter with an open mind to learning. Be ready to take action and become the strong, confident woman that is already inside you.

I never set out to be the Thought Leader and Guide that I have become in this world, but through my journey in life, this is where I am.

Let me share with you how it all began…

Being vulnerable and sharing my story was not something I thought I would ever be brave enough to do. I have always felt safer keeping my cards close to my chest and wearing a mask every single day. A mask I believed would keep me safe and loved, leading me to always be searching for that outside love and acceptance instead of looking within.

Wearing this mask every day became incredibly exhausting. It was relentlessly confusing for me to who I really was anymore. It came to a point when I looked in the mirror and didn't even recognise the shadow of who I really was and who I had become. It's actually quite a funny story about the day I realised I was ignoring the woman in the mirror. I had just moved into my brand-new house and had been living there for 3 days, using my bathroom twice daily for showers etc. It was not until the 3rd day I looked up and realised there wasn't even a mirror there! The builder had forgotten to put it in. I was that blind to who I had become; I wasn't even looking.

That afternoon my mirror arrived, and as I looked up, I noticed my eyes held darkness of complete lack of self-worth, self-confidence and self-respect. I was a stranger. The mask had dropped, and I was actually afraid of the woman I had become.

I lost who I was by choosing to stay in an emotionally abusive marriage for 7 years. By breaking all of my own personal boundaries, I lost all respect for myself because of the continued beating down of my confidence and worth most days. I not only lost myself, but I also lost my voice as well. A complete fear of speaking up and speaking my truth was embedded in my heart and soul, which I carried into my life for many years. The fear of being ridiculed and not saying the right thing. It was safer to just stay quiet. And that's exactly what I did.

This lack of all aspects of my internal self ricocheted throughout many areas of my life, affecting my friendships, my relationship with my family and the two businesses I was running at the time too.

I cut everyone out as I didn't know how to voice how I felt. I felt shame and embarrassed for who I had become. My businesses kept hitting a glass ceiling of earnings no matter how much effort and time I invested into "making it work". I was attracting people into my life that thrived on drama and cutting me down. I feared shining too bright and my then-husband ridiculing me and pulling me back down to where I was meant to be. I even experienced friends and clients going out of their way to pull me down.

I was afraid of what success would mean for me, my children and our life. I was afraid of the impact of the intense shame I felt on the life I was manifesting.

> Shame cannot survive being spoken. It cannot tolerate having words wrapped around it. What it craves is secrecy, silence and judgement. If you stay quiet, you stay in a lot of self-judgement.
> ~ Brene Brown

It was later I realised that I had no chance of breaking through this glass ceiling until I let go of the masculine energy and shame I was sitting in. You know the feeling...The continuous push, hustle and drive to survive. Always pushing, pushing and never taking the time to rest for fear of what that would mean. When you silence that beautiful, compassionate side of you to only allow self-judgment and ridicule, it is inevitable to see only blocks and glass ceilings. This continued push brought so much self-doubt and, dare I say, self-loathing into my own being. I just wasn't feeling authentic and true to who I was.

As my self-worth continued to plummet and I could see the domino effect starting to affect my small children, my relationships and my business, I knew something needed to shift, so I began to invest in myself. I wanted to learn how to let go of the fear of being seen and my greatest fear of success. I wanted to speak up about the shame I was experiencing, so other women did not have to go to the depths I had.

I soon realised that a big part of knowing how to let go and truly find my confidence was that I needed to re-learn how to comfortably sit with my driven masculine energy AND create the flow and groundedness of feminine energy. I learnt how to speak kindly to ME, prioritise my needs and become my own best friend. It was time to let go and fly!

I did this by investing 10 minutes daily to meditate and quiet my mind. My goodness, this is probably one of the most challenging tasks I have ever given myself. As a person who never wanted to "feel her feelings" and always had so much "busyness" running around her head, 10 minutes of quiet was definitely a challenge. However, by doing this, I was able to bring the feminine flow of compassion to myself by keeping the balance of masculine in that I gave myself a 30-day challenge to keep to 10 minutes of meditation every day. This small step created some of the biggest changes in my life.

I wanted to change. I invested and continue to invest in paid courses, coaches, deep healing, and personal development to support me in rising up out of the darkness of not recognising who I am anymore. To support me in becoming the thought leader I know I was born to be. I am a huge believer in investing in YOU if you want to rise up and make a difference.

Stepping into my feminine energy amplified my nurturing side of being more present and at the moment with my children. Enjoying them NOW instead of wishing theirs and my life away. I wanted to give my children a happier, safer, and more secure life. I wanted that for me too! Acknowledging the shame I felt gave me the strength to leave that emotionally abusive marriage and let go of my addiction to the drama of being put down not only by him but myself as well. This allowed me to step into the most beautiful Feminine power of compassion and understanding towards myself and towards my ex-husband and the journey he was on.

As I delved into my limiting beliefs and discovered the tools to show up authentically, I realised a big part of finding my confident, authentic voice meant it was time for me to balance my feminine and masculine energy. The very first tool I used and use with many of my clients to this day is asking myself the question, "Is this really true?". Then if the answer is NO, ask myself again, "then what is true at this moment?". Yes, this can be confronting at times. However, it can be extremely rewarding to bring you back into the present moment.

By creating this balance within, I was able to show up authentically without shame or self-judgement. Through healing within and finding a beautiful balance, I found I could more effortlessly stand up for my mission for women worldwide with a grounded and emotionally stable confidence that I had never experienced. I was able to become a shift changer for women, confidently knowing when a woman works with me, her life will transform, and she will manifest the body love and life of her dreams.

My beautiful client Mel is such a great example of what it looks like to invest in yourself and create healthy habits for YOU and YOUR lifestyle. Mel has invested in my 8-week transformation program twice and continues to thrive in her body confidence and life. She first invested to create healthy habits, so she could juggle her career and be a mum of 2 young girls. She achieved this and more, losing over 10kg, committing to regular movement with my online community, and shifting her mindset and nutrition habits that felt effortless. When Mel came back for her 2nd round of my program, she came with a different goal; wanting to find direction and confidence in where she was going with her career and, again, how that would impact her family. Throughout the program, Mel focused more on the mindset component of learning how to focus on HER needs and what would bring her joy and happiness while still being an incredible mum and partner too. Since completing the second round of my Body Conscious to Body Confidence, Mel is now studying law, still working in her current career, making time for her exercise, fuelling her body for optimal energy while still having the time and energy for her family. Creating sustainable habits and learning to shift your mindset is a game changer. For you, for your life and for all those surrounding you too!

Leanne first met me at one of my speaking events. I was presenting on an Empowerment Panel on International Women's Day. Empowering women to step into their balanced Feminine Power is an absolute passion of mine. I believe that with more powerful women in our world, the more our world will be led with empathy and compassion.

Anyhow, enough about me...let's get back to Leanne. She first came to me to find her happiness again, to set goals for herself and believe she could achieve them. Leanne is the driving force behind her husband's construction company and embarking on her career path, becoming a clinical therapist herself. When I first met Leanne, she was very much in her masculinity, feeling like she was not in her authenticity or even her true power. She didn't recognise the woman in the mirror anymore. She had become a stranger to herself. As we worked together, Leanne and I discovered that her lack of feminine energy was her greatest block to showing up as her true authentic self. Leanne's masculine energy showed up as setting many rules in her life. Even though the action-orientated traits benefited her in many ways, she lacked in her creative flow and intuition of the feminine. I supported Leanne in letting go of limiting beliefs and bringing in new resourceful beliefs to drive her forward in her career and life. Leanne is now listening to her inner knowing. She truly loves the woman she is and respects her deeply. By doing this work, Leanne has set up her very own office with a beautiful feminine flair and is ready to start her new career path with feminine confidence, drive, and masculine leadership. She has found her voice with her husband and is now networking with other women effortlessly. Something she was shied away from before we worked together. Leanne and I continue to work together 1:1 as she continues to rise. It is truly exciting to walk beside her, empower her and help her remove the blocks that hold her back from the next level of her life and business.

Learning how to return to self and put yourself first is a big part of gaining authentic confidence in business and life. My client Nicole first joined my 8-week transformation program to find herself again after years of juggling #mumlife, working and having a sick child. She had forgotten how to do that. She was walking through life on autopilot and feeling stuck in the life she was living. Since completing Body Conscious to Body, Confidence, Nicole is now working in her dream career, studying and feeling more confident than ever before. By adding in small, simple steps, Nicole could love her body again and feel confident in who she was, allowing her to stand up and ask for what she deserved in life. This shift in Nicole not only impacted her life but those around her. "Since working with Danni, my family is so much more connected, filled with so much fun and laughter", ~ Nicole.

Like Mel and Nicole, many of my clients effortlessly move from body conscious and hiding who they truly are to body confidence and achieving goals they never dreamed of in business and life by using my 8 Week transformation program. I invite you to find out more details about this program on my website.

It continues to be such an incredible domino effect when you work on YOU; everyone around you is impacted in such a positive way.

This is why it is my vision of impact to eradicate self-loathing in women worldwide. I believe when women love and respect themselves completely, our world can be led with the nurturing traits it takes to connect to human beings in a meaningful and fulfilling way. Imagine our world filled with leaders embracing the flow of balanced feminine energy, leading with compassion, kindness, and empathy because they're already giving this love and compassion to themselves!

My genius is presenting holistic wellness workshops and programs on empowering entrepreneurial women to harness their femininity in a masculine-dominant world. I love to work with companies including Ausmumpreneur, The Corporate Escapists & many wellness communities that hold a culture of support and understanding that once we empower the women, their lives are improved and those around them, including their partners, children and friends. I believe it is a domino effect so needed in our world to create positive change to a more optimal health-based society.

This most certainly is not the end of my journey. At times it certainly feels like it is just the beginning. A journey of empowering women by showing them how to be true to themselves, fearlessly go within and create space for themselves without guilt. When women do this, they can achieve anything in life, in business, and in relationships. A woman in her true authenticity with deep self-love, self-respect and self-acceptance will always be and show up with unstoppable confidence.

It is my Vision to be the thought leader for women's empowerment, body confidence and authenticity. To be impacting tens of thousands of humans all over the world through my keynote speaking/motivational speaking, transformational programs and integrated wellness retreats. I will be the leader in eradicating self-loathing in women worldwide so that the world, businesses and our families can be filled with compassion, kindness and optimal emotional intelligence. My purpose in life is to support humans to rise through speaking, empowering and inspiring, and I would love to offer my expertise at your next event.

Making change begins with us. It is time to shift the dialogue and recognise the importance of mental health, especially for the women in our world trying to do everything and be everything for everyone around them. It is important we are aware of the importance of healthy outlets to empower our minds and hearts. Building strategies around being able to shift this is the way.

We are the change. My wish for you is to embrace the balance of feminine and masculine energy to gain grounded confidence that will allow you to show up authentically in business and in life. Let the adventure begin xx.

It is confidence in our bodies, minds & spirits that allows us to keep looking for new adventures.

~ Oprah Winfrey

About the Author

Danni Vee is a Speaker, Author and Mind Body Mentor. As a certified Neuro-Linguistic Practitioner, an integrated holistic wellness Specialist and Certified Fitness & Nutrition Coach, Danni has been a passionate leader in the Wellness Industry for over 14 years now and has grown a motivated and loyal community of thousands.

Danni coaches ambitious entrepreneurs and business leaders who lack confidence and feel like they've tried almost everything to transform their minds and body so that they can show up with true authenticity and effortlessly reach their biggest goals with unstoppable confidence. Danni's mission is to eradicate self-loathing worldwide so that our world can be led by compassionate leaders creating a domino effect of peace and harmony throughout the world. Danni is available to speak and offers programs to suit the needs of a diverse range of companies and individuals.

Website: www.dannivee.com
Instagram: @danniveecoach
LinkedIn: www.linkedin.com/in/danni-vee-empowerment-motivational-coach

Camilla Ward

Bringing out The Creative Voice Within...

Without a song or a dance?
What are we?
So I say thank you for the music for giving it to me
(Thank you for the Music-Abba The Album-1977)

Song 1 - *(From Voices of Impact - Cam's Playlist- Spotify)*

Losing My Voice

These lyrics of Abba still hold as much meaning to me as they did all those years ago in the seventies. When I first heard that song, I never realised how the finding, losing and recreation of my own voice would influence my life, my career paths, and those around me.

As I write this chapter, I think back to the veranda of our family homestead. There was always music and conversation blaring from the kitchen radio with underlying static tones which resonated in my ears. Usually, it was ABC with programs like The Country Hour, a daily ritual for farmers to connect with others in the rural community about what was happening in the markets, the stock exchange and the latest agricultural developments.

It aired at noon daily when my father came in for his cooked lunch, a break from being in the paddocks or fixing something which seemed to be a forever ongoing practice.

If my mother was in the kitchen, it was tuned into ABC classic FM, her reminiscing about her previous life as a professional violinist and teacher in the city before meeting the love of her life, my father and moving to country NSW. My days as a child, in the beginning, were carefree and growing up in the country was an absolute blessing. However, as the eighties came, our household changed dramatically. My father's health was failing with his ongoing cancer. Interest rates were soaring, affecting all livelihoods on the land and increasing the stress and weight of responsibility for my mother.

At this time, I watched as my mother, who was considerably younger than my father, take over the farm's management and day-to-day running. My younger brother and I didn't grasp the magnitude of what was happening, but I would lose myself in music as an escape.

This is my journey as a Playlist.

Song 2 - Xanadu - Olivia Newton-John (1982)

Olivia's voice swept me away from the harshness of my reality to a place with colour, neon lights and roller skates. The freedom I felt as I glided up and down my veranda imagining being her.

When my father finally succumbed to cancer the following year, music was the only time I could really express and connect with myself.

I was growing up in a period of time in a society where compliance and being a good girl were valued and validated. I believed I always had to do the right thing and say what was expected of me; I was always quite an outgoing child. However, sometimes my personality was a bit too much. So, elders and peers advised me to tone it down and not be so much ME.

So, I would then channel that energy into singing and playing music. Skating up and down on that veranda, singing my heart out, I was in my happy place. I could escape to where everything was beautiful, and life was a musical, and I was the central character creating my own storyline. I often felt unheard and overwhelmed. Through an adult's significant violation of trust early in my life, I found myself not sharing and being fully present with others emotionally. This led to disconnection and disassociation. At times, impulsivity nearly led to severe and potentially dangerous consequences in my quest to feel something, anything. I could only feel my emotions when I was singing, playing music, and acting. In these moments, I felt safe and powerful.

Song 3 - True Colours - Cyndi Lauper (1986)

Cindy Lauper was my very first concert experience. I was 13 and had never seen anyone with so much vitality and musicality other than in classical concerts and operas with which I had grown up. Her eclectic dress sense, voice, and energy. It was just electric. From that moment, I was drawn to singers and performers like that. So impulsively, as I tend to be, I dived headfirst into discovering all I could about the 80s music scene.

This was when I first experienced the elitism and music shaming that existed within the world of music, and the quest for perfectionism, which I believed was required to be a 'real musician'; it was a bar I felt I couldn't quite reach, and this set me on a course of my inner critic relentlessly judging and critiquing my every performance and rehearsal.

I was constantly searching for my voice but did not know what it was or what I wanted to say. That expectation that I would do something great always weighed extremely heavily on me and led to anxiety and depression in later years when I could not live up to my then-belief of what a successful life was. The feeling that I had to justify through performance to receive the validation, to show myself and others that I was worthy. Winning awards and being chosen to perform was the only time I acknowledged I had succeeded. In recent years, I realised I could sing for myself without a set prescribed outcome or audience.

Song 4 - Take on Me - Aha (1985)

I still listen with the same joy and anticipation to this song today, taking me to my happy place. In my first year of boarding school, at age 12 in the big city of Sydney, I played this song endlessly. I was very grateful for the lifelong friends I made and the experiences I had at school. When I couldn't express my emotions in words, I'd search for a song with specific lyrics and sing it out. I had ongoing illnesses as a teenager and so found solace there. There was always a song to suit my mood at the time. However, the elitism and musical shaming I witnessed again found me asking the question, who decides who is musical? Aren't we all?

Song 5 - Holding out for a Hero - Bonnie Tyler (1984)

It cemented my longing for a hero who would come and rescue me. Unfortunately, I never felt I was strong enough to save myself. I was an avid Love Song Dedication Radio listener. I spent many hours when I should have been studying, calling up the station, putting on funny voices and requesting songs for fictional boyfriends and husbands who I missed due to interstate jobs or incarceration.

Song 6 - Come on, Eileen - Dexy Midnight Runners (1982)

My grandmother was named Eileen, a talented pianist and violist, and I always resonated with that song after her death in my teens. Not that I ever would've called her Eileen, of course. She was always Grandma to me. Exploring contemporary culture through music and voice has played an ongoing focus in my life. Countdown was one of my absolute favourite TV shows because we only had ABC on the farm until I was about seven or eight. I was glued to the TV set every Sunday night. I'd have my tape recorder ready to record those new up-and-coming top 10 chart stoppers as a mix tape whilst trying to quieten the family background chatter.

Why am I telling you all this? Well, I suppose, in a way, it's showing you how my perceptions had been formed and guiding me to songwriters, performers, and artists, to help me find my voice and then support others to find theirs. I was always drawn to anything that allowed me to express myself outside my persona. It came quickly to me to play a character, sing a song and embody that performance. But to ask me about myself, I had no voice. I did not believe I had a voice to contribute with. So, my teenage years ended.

Song 7 - It's Only the Beginning

It's only the beginning, but I've already gone and lost my mind.
Deborah Conway (1991)

These lyrics spoke to me. I now had the freedom I'd never experienced before; I partied. I danced. I stopped singing. Why? I think because I couldn't connect to it anymore. And so, I began the journey in my twenties. Burnout was inevitable, and it came in the second year of university. Heading back to the farm gave me time to really think. What was I doing with my life? I had enrolled as a teacher at uni. I really wanted to be an actor, but I was advised that a teaching job was a more stable choice of career, and I did not believe I could do it on my own. I think I was drawn to teaching because it was like acting in a way. I always loved the connection and community, not the endless administration side, but getting in a room where I could communicate with my students. So back to university I went, finished the degree. And then, I started teaching and searching for my voice.

Song 8 - Galileo

How long 'til my soul gets it right can any human being ever reach that kind of light

I call on the resting soul of Galileo, King of night vision, King of insight -Indigo Girls (1992)

My first position in Sydney was at a girls' school, and again I met lifelong friends and colleagues. However, due to my unresolved childhood trauma, I would get to a stage when I was under extreme pressure or stress; it would become so overwhelming and impossible that I would become ill and leave my workplace. It wasn't until years later that I realised repeated behaviour patterns through therapy. It was my body trying to protect me from myself. I'd always said that I would teach for three years in Australia and then head overseas to the UK. And I did that. And those two years were the happiest of my life at that time. I think because I was a nobody. The freedom to create my own story and experiences was liberating.

Song 9 - You Only Get What You Give - New Radicals (1998)

I came back and started The Creative Voice Studio. Why? I had this opportunity to see education not just in Australia but around the world. I wanted to be involved with supporting others to bring out their creative voice within a system I believed was broken for our children. So, I went from London back to Quirindi, the rural town where I had spent many happy years growing up. I was so fortunate and grateful to be embraced by the community. I was able to run the studio locally, offering singing, speech, and drama lessons from school-aged children to adults who wanted to express themselves in an inclusive and safe environment.

I connected with others by combining my intuition with skills, techniques, and healing modalities I had experienced here and overseas. And I loved it.

Recreating My Own Voice

I met my now husband back in my hometown; it wasn't instant love at first sight, more of a slow burn which continues to this day. He is my best mate, partner, and father to our two incredible humans. We have been through so many challenges and joys together over the past 22 years. He supports my passion and the evolving path of The Creative Voice Studio, and I am grateful every day for his love, laughter, companionship and cooking.

Sydney was calling me back, so I enrolled in TAFE, completed Workplace Training while teaching, and knew my life was heading in a different direction, but I wasn't sure which path. It was then I had my first life breakdown or, as I now say, breakthrough. I was confronted with a situation I did not know how to handle emotionally and could not process. And as a result, I was diagnosed with depression and anxiety, so I left my teaching job and my students. I went back home to the farm, to my partner, to recuperate and regain my strength.

I felt that I had failed, was broken, and was not enough. I could not control the tide of big emotions that refused to be silent inside me anymore. I gradually got stronger. And with the love of my partner, family, and friends, I continued developing the studio. We married and moved to Brisbane. And for the first time, I could work exclusively in the performing arts world.

The birth of my eldest child at the end of this time signified a new song in my life playlist.

She was born on my birthday, what a present. After living there for three years, we decided to move back closer to family. So we packed up our house with a three-week-old baby and moved to Dubbo, Western NSW. If I'd thought about it, logically, I wouldn't have done it. But the impending overwhelmingness of having a child and being so far away from family brought me back to regional NSW, where I still am today. Like with my husband, there was definitely a transition period going from the bright lights of Brisbane to a stay-at-home mother in a country town with a husband that travelled for work. The day-to-day grind I found extremely difficult. It was not surprising. I was diagnosed with postnatal depression.

Song 10-Nightminds

I will learn to breathe this ugliness you see, so we can both be there, and we can both share the dark... Missy Higgins (2004)

I still believed in the studio. I still thought that we should bring out our creative voice, but how could I do that with a new baby, my overwhelming feelings of inadequacy in a different town, and my new home? It took me quite a few years to challenge my subconscious limiting beliefs, and using my voice again was instrumental. I played my piano, constantly singing to my daughter nonsense songs I'd make up. What really saved me in those dark moments was carpool karaoke. Taking a moment, sometimes child-free, to jump into the car, windows down, singing my heart out. I started working again in the studio and teaching in the community part-time. But then, before I knew it, baby number two was on the way; my beautiful boy was born prematurely at 28 weeks at Dubbo Base Hospital. Not quite the calm birthing that I had envisaged for him. However, thanks to the neonatal care he received, we all returned to Dubbo after a lengthy 5 months in Sydney.

Those next few years were taken up with caring for the children, early intervention for my son, teaching when I was able to and listening to music. I had not performed publicly for many years, as I felt I couldn't connect with my voice. When I spoke to other mums in mother's groups about singing, they would say, " Oh, I'd love to sing, " but I was told I couldn't sing. Or I was told to mime in the choir" This so frustrated me because we all have an instrument; our voice is like our fingerprint, unique and to be used as a deep source of expression and experience, not just entertainment and education.

Another story a mother told me was she never sang happy birthday to her child because she was so embarrassed by her voice and the perceived judgement she felt. That upset me so much to hear. How do we initially communicate and connect with our children? With our babies? We sing to soothe and reassure them.

This conversation was becoming more common, and a fire was now burning inside me that I could not ignore. This was about creating my own manifesto for music and living it daily.

Clients often come to me initially for specific singing or public speaking challenges; however, what they often find is a CVS (Creative Voice Session) is beneficial in all areas of their life.

After the last couple of years of isolation and disconnection, they are searching for a connection to themselves, and the voice is instrumental in this.

There are five strengths I bring to my life and work in the studio each day.

1. Connectedness-I connect my clients with their voice and a part of themselves that has been hidden, suppressed and shamed at times.

2. Positivity-I love to have fun with my clients, and my enthusiasm can be contagious.

3. Strategy-I find alternative ways to achieve outcomes with each client I work with.

4. Empathy- I can tune into the mood of an individual or group. My aim is to inspire others to be themselves by connecting with their voice.

5. Individualisation- I am skilled at working out how different people work together, building on their strengths. My experience as an educator, theatre producer/director and musical conductor has given me invaluable insight into this.

> It takes a village to raise a child.
> ~ Proverb

I am so grateful for the following mentors I have in my life:

Melanie from Speaking Styles has been instrumental in finding my voice and sharing it on social media, so I now work with

clients all over the world

Rebel from The Rural Woman Cooperative- "Bloom where you are planted' I aim to do that daily in my community.

Petrea King-Quest for Life. Providing a beautiful space where I can just heal, be and reconnect with myself.

Allison Davis The Magic and Medicine of Music. Your manifesto for Music and this program has forever changed me.

Lisa Corduff: For supporting the business side. I now financially value myself and my expertise.

I believe our voice is one of our greatest tools for self-expression, emotional release, advocacy and empowerment.
~ Allison Davis-The Magic and Medicine of Music

About the Author

Camilla Ward is the founder/owner of The Creative Voice Studio, specialising in singing, public speaking, and consultation in the NSW Arts sector. Born in Quirindi, Camilla now lives in Dubbo, where she has run her successful business for over 15 years whilst raising her family and singing "carpool karaoke".

Camilla has inspired hundreds of children and adults of all ages, using unique techniques developed over many years of working with communities and organisations in Australia and overseas. Camilla was awarded The Dubbo Electorate Local Woman of the Year 2019 for her community contribution to the Arts and is regularly invited to present her story.

Camilla loves living in regional NSW and is found at one of her many favourite coffee shops having a "meeting" and connecting with her community. Her favourite pastime is performing "Live at Five" on her Facebook page with her piano or keyboard in her signature slippers.

Email: creativevoicestudio@gmail.com
Facebook: www.facebook.com/creativevoicestudio
Website: www.thecreativevoicestudio.com.au

Rhonda Whiteley

In the fight that I will win, to see the joys life can bring.
There is one goal I have set, on this journey, I will get.
It is simple that I know, from deep within, where energies flow.
Four little ways say it all, release the fear and hear me call.
Be free, be me.

In 2007, those words were the catalyst for change as I accepted a new beginning using 'be free be me' as my mantra. Little did I know the journey of self-transformation was only beginning and would take more than a decade to complete the journey.

You are more than a survivor, you have been transformed..

~ Eleanor Brown

How did it all begin! During my childhood, I experienced abuse that had me searching for some answers. What was I doing wrong? How could I be better? Why wasn't I good enough? No matter how much I tried to keep the peace, I always felt that what I did was never going to be enough. Over time I started to block the feelings and didn't know the impact those blockages would have on my life until many years later.

Abuse comes in many forms, and the effects of the abuse and traumatic experiences may not surface for many years, and at times the intense emotional feelings may reveal themselves in unexpected moments when you feel in total control of your life at that present time.

This is my story and if you can relate to my experiences and they make you feel less alone and afraid to reach out for help, then putting pen to paper is worth more than these words could express. Please be gentle with yourself during any recovery process and have a support crew around you, as it is not something you need to face alone.

Understanding how the conscious and subconscious mind works has enabled me to sift through the recollection of events and file away those that may have been altered during the passing of time. It doesn't mean I pretend they aren't real but review how I feel about them now. Getting back to the story…

To be honest, I don't remember a lot about my childhood, and occasionally I will remember a moment and check in with my siblings about the event. It used to cause very unsettled feelings, but now I know I will remember when I am strong enough to accept the memories, or they are no longer relevant.

As I moved into adulthood, the insecurities and low self-esteem started to reveal themselves. No matter what I was doing, self-doubt was always there, and old questions would consume my waking thoughts. What if I'm not good enough? What if I make a mistake? What if no one likes me? and on and on. I struggled to assert my feelings, beliefs or preferences, acceptance became part of my life, and slowly, it was consuming my every waking hour. Being torn apart internally by not following my beliefs and values impacted my health. Sleepless nights, migraines, food intolerances and body aches were part of my daily life; I thought I just had to accept them and move on.

> Believe in Yourself
> You are your greatest asset, there is nothing you can't do. No one can keep you from dreaming, only you can stop them coming true.
> Your achievements are determined by the desire that you possess. There is no better feeling than the feeling of success.
> Believe that who you are, believe that what you do. Is not a quirk of fate, it's strictly up to you!
> ~ Author unknown

As I wasn't ready to process my past, I wanted to escape the childhood memories and immersed myself in new beginnings, and a relationship soon developed. I got married and started this new adventure with absolute commitment and gusto. After a short time, the needing to keep the peace and not speaking my mind resurfaced, and cracks started to appear. The family then became my focus as I silently tried to keep myself mentally healthy by pushing the childhood memories deeper and deeper.

Personal development became my go-to place as I emersed myself in books, seminars and courses. A huge influencer at the time was Anthony Robbins; where in 2002, I attended an event in Sydney, stepped out of my comfort zone, walked across hot coals, and the realisation that pushing my childhood memories down had blocked way more than the feelings associated with experiencing abuse.

We did an exercise where we had to imagine sitting in a big, coloured bubble floating over our timeline. There were a few issues with the exercise. First, I couldn't decide on the colour of my bubble...what was my favourite colour? Second, my timeline was black; there was nothing to see until I got close to the current time. I was a bit disheartened and thought perhaps there was a reason I couldn't remember my past and should leave it in the past.

The next exercise gave some comfort when we had to float over a point in our timeline and recreate a memory. This image came through to me of a lady walking along the beach with two children. She was dressed in a white soft flowing dress with her shoulder-length hair being blown by the gentle sea air. It wasn't really someone I recognised, but somehow I felt connected to this person. The memory was so comforting, and I couldn't help but feel I had somehow blocked so much of my past that I couldn't remember this event at all.

Over time I learned to accept the memory, and the exercise became my perfect day meditation. As I settled into bed, before I could drift off to sleep, I would start to plan my perfect day from the moment I opened my eyes in the morning to when I went to bed. It was like watching a movie as I didn't know what was going to happen. Over a decade later, I still haven't gotten to the end of my day – I drift off to sleep well before that time. I've tried to start part way through the day, but that has never worked.

Gradually I was finding the real me and understanding that what I was doing was not where I needed to be. I struggled to stay in a job for more than 3 months as once I was expected to know the role, the panic attacks would start, I would doubt myself, and mistakes would show up. The time had come to make the decision to leave my marriage.

In my dreams
In my dreams, I met them all and told them how I felt,
told them I don't understand these cards I was dealt
I felt the anger in my voice, never heard that before,
I knew right then I had to forgive to heal right to the core.

My heart was pounding & my breathing fast. I saw them fade away,
I knew this time I had crossed that bridge and was "finally free" I say.
I woke up with a smile and felt the peace within,
I now keep the feeling close to my heart for the healing to begin.
There will be times when the pain returns, and I know just what to do,
return to my dreams when I stood my ground and said, "now it's up to you".

Not knowing where to go, who to confide in or what I was feeling started to consume me. I had maintained a survival level of existence for over a year, and it was becoming obvious that I was no longer able to manage. Sleep was deprived, food was no longer on my high priority list, and I could see no way out. I then gave up on life and tried to end it.

The choice was made to seek help. Support from my counsellor, friends and family was more valuable than I could have imagined. I continued to work on my mental and emotional health, knowing that this would be paramount in my recovery. There were times when it was very hard, like opening pandora's box and not knowing what was inside. It hasn't been easy but has been worth every moment and everything I have discovered about myself. We can sometimes be scared about change, especially when we may have been that way for a long time. The unknown can be very scary as well – what if this isn't the right way, how do I know what to do or how to make decisions? I realised how much I had been controlled, and now it was time to find me.

Holistic health has shown how negative thoughts and feelings can create illness or dis-ease in the body.

Some months later, I made a decision that changed my life from then on. I decided to take control of my life and live it my way. Just existing was no longer an option; I needed a reason to live and one that I was excited about. That may sound simple, but living for so long to please others was the norm; I had to start doing things because they lit the fire within, and at first, it was a case of trial and error to find out what excited me. Creating a vision board or list of experiences that I wanted was a great start. What did I used to enjoy? What made time disappear? Or a phrase I used in my workshops is, what makes your heart sing? Going back to what I enjoyed as a child, I started exploring art again. I was very self-conscious and wanted every stroke to be perfect. It was hard to relax at first and let the creative juices flow. Slowly I got back my creative mojo, and time would disappear when I immersed myself in the creative moments, and I would relax and forget the challenges I was facing.

Journaling in a few different forms became an important part of my daily practice. I used written journaling to get stuff out of my head, so I could sleep, gratitude to focus on the good in my life and creative journaling to express emotions, thoughts or feelings creatively. None of those practices was to be reviewed later; it was for the moment. All the little changes started to gather momentum and before long other areas of my life were improving. This was not happening overnight, the changes were gradual, and over weeks, months, or in some cases, years, I started to feel different...I started to feel me. That feeling was forever changing and developing as I grew and changed and grew some more.

I continued to grow and develop my self-confidence, and an interest in the human body developed. Originally my thoughts were of being a life coach, where I could support people through life changes as they recover from trauma. Something didn't feel right...how could I be a life coach if I couldn't even go to the dentist. As it turned out, I needed to go to the dentist; it had been 30 years since my previous appointment. I was scared of being in a vulnerable position that I couldn't escape; I was scared of not being able to scream for help. My sensible side knows that a dentist needs to look in your mouth to help, but the scared side of me couldn't get other images out of my head. The mental work began. It took 6 months of visualization, meditation and exposing myself to smaller uncomfortable situations to turn off the fight and flight response. The day came, and I comfortably walked in, sat in the chair and had my tooth repaired. I walked outside and knew that what I had taught myself was worth sharing; it was a total feeling of euphoria. The feelings I felt couldn't be put into words, the fear was part of me for 30 + years, and I had put that to bed and learnt how to overcome those debilitating feelings that stopped me from doing what I needed to do for my personal health.

Now I could work on what I was passionate about – helping other women.

Overcoming ideals and thoughts from others was also difficult. It appeared that I was always changing and never staying with something for very long. There are times in our lives when believing in ourselves can be challenging and, at times, even seem impossible. Social media, television, and even family and friends can inadvertently plant small seeds in our minds that quickly grow into weeds, aka unwanted thoughts, that seem to change our thinking or beliefs. We no longer value our thoughts but believe in what others are saying. It was time to trust my own feelings and do what I knew was right for me.

That was a light bulb moment; I wanted to be a healer. At the time, I didn't realise that I could combine art and healing modalities. I started my holistic well-being study journey in 2017 mainly for my own recovery, and my passion for art and holistic well-being came together in 2020 after completing the further study. Now a meditation teacher, holistic counsellor, Holistic Integrated Creative Arts Therapist and Chakradance Facilitator, supporting women through their journey of recovery is a dream come true. My daily practice includes meditation, journaling and time in nature with other practices that are maintained weekly. If I shelve the practices for a short time, I start to feel heavy and know I need to get back to them.

Wanting to share my story and help other women, I felt the need to improve my confidence when speaking to others. Holding workshops and classes was a regular occurrence, and although a bit uncomfortable at times, it wasn't too daunting. Taking it to the next level was another story. Did I want to do this or continue playing it small?

To help with difficult decisions, I would return to visualization and imagine myself on stage or doing whatever I was considering. After a short period of time, it was evident that speaking on stage was something I wanted to do; I felt it was the best way to share my story and inspire women to grow. Being quiet-spoken and even more so around people, I had to move way out of my comfort zone to overcome this fear. The vision of sharing my story was so strong that public speaking had to be next on my agenda. Using the same principle as I did for my dentist visit, I prepared for Toastmasters. Then a few years later I was invited to participate in an event - Queensland Mental Health Week guest speaker in 2021. There was no doubt I was nervous to stand on stage and share my story, but at the same time, I felt honoured to have this opportunity.

The steps to establishing a business began, and as I decided on the services, the business name revealed itself. Business names evolved, starting with Be True Be You life coaching, then Free to Be You and finally…Inner Pathways Education was born - an online business supporting women through their journey of recovery with workshops, e-books and one on one support. Programs have been developed to further impart my experiences and skills to the women who become part of the Inner Pathways community.

Breaking the Chains: 7 steps to free yourself after abuse and trauma e-book and program is a compilation of the tools I used during my recovery then followed, Power to Freedom program brings all the life lessons together to create your vision plan for holistic wellbeing and mental health journey.

Both programs can be summed up into one sentence:

Break the chains of the past and step into your power to freedom

Even reading that now gives me goosebumps – my vision has become a reality.

Be True Be You
Eight years ago, I tried to end it all,
I struggled in silence no friends did I call.
How did my spirit get so terribly low?
I still ask that question but need to let it go.
Today my life is different, and I enjoy every gift,
the time I share with others always gives me a lift.
I treasure my family and hold those feelings close,
there are many things I've learned, but one I use the most.
Be true, be you.

What I want for you is to provide you with the tools and inspiration that are perfect for you to create the life of your dreams away from the effects of trauma and abuse. Join the community of Inner Pathways Education and be supported during your healing journey. Together we can end violence against women...that is my dream and is why I am passionate about helping you be the best version of yourself and inspiring people around you to change.

Breaking the Chains
Invisible chains tie you down
Harsh words, hugs withheld
No friends, scars unseen
Feelings shut down
Time for change
Release
Tears
Heart open
Forgiving self
Creating, igniting
Friendships, healing
Kind words...comforting
Broken chains, freedom to be me

I look forward to working with you and supporting you through your healing journey.

Let's begin your journey to freedom together.

About the Author

Rhonda is the Founder of Inner Pathways Educations, guiding women to uncover their strengths through Breaking the Chains and Power to Freedom online programs. Drawn to meditation, Chakradance and holistic health by her own health challenges, Rhonda has discovered the healing and therapeutic benefits of the practices.

Rhonda is passionate about helping clients realise their own potential and achieve vibrant health by dramatically creating healthier, more balanced lives. She will help you discover your inner strength and provide guidance to release old patterns and beliefs. Practising meditation and holistic well-being, Rhonda has found balance in her life. She is a creative, understanding person who loves to learn and share her knowledge with others to help them uncover their true self. Rhonda has an Advanced Diploma in Meditation Teaching & Holistic Human Development, HICAT Diploma (Holistic Integrated Creative Arts Therapist) and is a Chakradance Facilitator.

Email: rhonda@innerpathwayseducation.com.au
Website: www.innerpathwayseducation.com.au
Facebook: facebook.com/innerpathways

Voices of Impact

www.ingramcontent.com/pod-product-compliance
Lightning Source LLC
Chambersburg PA
CBHW050304010526
44107CB00055B/2101